IMAGES
of America

SEABROOK FARMS

IMAGES
of America

SEABROOK FARMS

Cheryl L. Baisden

ARCADIA
PUBLISHING

Published by Arcadia Publishing
Charleston SC, Chicago IL, Portsmouth NH, San Francisco CA

Library of Congress Catalog Card Number: 2007923655

For all general information contact Arcadia Publishing at:
Telephone 843-853-2070
Fax 843-853-0044
E-mail sales@arcadiapublishing.com
For customer service and orders:
Toll-Free 1-888-313-2665

Visit us on the Internet at www.arcadiapublishing.com

This book is dedicated to John "Jack" Martin Seabrook,
who served as president of Seabrook Farms during its zenith in the
1950s. It was Jack Seabrook who had the foresight to gather displaced
workers from around the world to establish a global village that
provided innumerable families an opportunity to start new lives,
forge new friendships, and gather memories to last a lifetime.
Together with his father, C. F. Seabrook, and brothers Belford
and Courtney, Jack helped revolutionize farming and the produce
marketplace. His remarkable accomplishments are gratefully
memorialized in this impressive selection of historical photographs.

CONTENTS

ACKNOWLEDGMENTS

This book would not have been possible without the assistance of the Seabrook Educational and Cultural Center (SECC) staff and volunteers, who were kind enough to provide access to their extraordinary photograph collection and guidance in accurately portraying Seabrook's remarkable history. All of the photographs in this historical collection were provided by the SECC, which opened in 1994. Committed to preserving the unique history of Seabrook Farms as a place where people of differing races and cultures were given the chance to start new lives, the SECC is located in the Upper Deerfield Township Municipal Building and is open to the public for tours and research. The assistance of John "Jack" Seabrook, who reviewed this book for accuracy prior to publication, also is graciously acknowledged.

INTRODUCTION

The enterprise that would one day become the Seabrook Farms empire began humbly in 1893, when Arthur P. (A. P.) Seabrook, a small tenant farmer who raised vegetables and sold his harvest from a huckster wagon in Bridgeton, purchased a nearby 57-acre farm in what is now Upper Deerfield. But while A. P. was content tending to his little corner of Cumberland County, his son Charles Franklin (C. F.) Seabrook had other ideas.

Under C. F.'s leadership, as well as the visionary efforts of sons Belford, C. Courtney, and John "Jack," Seabrook Farms's holdings grew to 20,000 acres (making it the largest vegetable farm in the world), and farmers from four states came under contract to help the South Jersey company generate enough vegetables and fruit to feed its massive processing plant.

It was the company's revolutionary technique for quick-freezing fresh fruits and vegetables that first won Seabrook Farms national recognition, changing the way America eats. But while growing, processing, packaging, and distributing frozen produce for the likes of Birdseye and dozens of lesser-known labels, as well as its own, brought Seabrook fame, it was the company's innovations in farming technique, production, and employment practices that earned it a lasting place in the annals of the agriculture industry. Between its incorporation in 1913 and its shift in ownership in 1959, the Seabrook Farms Company—with its four subsidiaries of Seabrook Farming Corporation (growing), Deerfield Packing Company (processing and quick-freezing), Cumberland Warehouse Corporation (refrigerated storage), and Cumberland Auto and Truck Corporation (transport), as well as C. F.'s personally owned construction company, Seabrook Engineering Corporation—changed farming and food processing forever. In the process, the company changed the face of southern New Jersey, bringing remarkable cultural diversity to the rural region.

Although the farm laborers no longer toil in the fields, the processing plant no longer hums around the clock, and the once-bustling town center has been absorbed into the region's still-rural landscape, the company's spirit remains alive in the hearts of the thousands of families who sowed the seeds for new lives in the fertile fields called Seabrook.

One

A Family of Visionaries

"As a farmer," Jack Seabrook once wrote, "[my father] was distinguished by a strong dislike of dirt." Oddly enough, the man who would one day command the largest vegetable farm in the world, was, in fact, a reluctant farmer. But C. F. Seabrook's agricultural aversion, along with the talent and insight of his three sons, actually served the industry well. Beginning with a teenaged experiment that ultimately altered irrigation practices for farmers around the world, the engineering enthusiast who dropped out of school at the age of 12 envisioned farming as an industrial operation rather than an agricultural venture. His sons followed suit, and working together they grew Seabrook Farms into a giant in both the farming and the food processing industries.

In its relatively short 56-year history, the Seabrook Farms Company methodically built a business like no other, and in the process became an innovator in frozen food development, overhead irrigation systems, agricultural assembly line production, and scientific farming techniques. Even Seabrook's workforce philosophy made history—seeking out and employing workers from both around the corner and around the world happy to trade a life of economic depression, war, or political strife for the chance to start new lives in rural South Jersey.

From the unique design of its company town to its scientifically calculated planting schedules, Seabrook Farms's long list of firsts was the direct result of a family of visionaries.

English-born A. P. Seabrook, a truck farmer whose father worked for *New York Tribune* editor and abolitionist Horace Greeley, unwittingly planted the seeds for the Seabrook Farms empire in 1893, when he purchased his own small farm in what was then Deerfield Township. Over the years, A. P. made a comfortable living with the 57-acre Minch Farm.

A. P.'s son, C. F. Seabrook, had no desire to follow in his father's footsteps, dreaming instead of a career in engineering. In 1911, he purchased his father's farm, incorporated in 1913, and ultimately blended the two professions into one, transforming the modest operation into what *Life* magazine dubbed "the biggest vegetable factory on earth" in 1955, by amassing thousands of acres of farmland and building a sprawling factory complex and village.

Ironically, C. F. was a natural when it came to agriculture. In 1907, at the age of 14, he designed the earliest portable sprinkler system in the country after hearing about a Danish farmer's overhead irrigation experiments. By installing a single pipe with punched holes over a celery bed, he increased crop production by an estimated 300 percent and quickly realized the system's potential. Above is a view of the overhead system used at Seabrook Farms until 1935. Below, field workers carry a later portable watering system into the field. Today's portable irrigation systems are still based on C. F.'s designs, although they now rely on wheels for maneuverability rather than manpower.

By 1921, Seabrook Farms had expanded to include 4,000 acres of farmland, 10 acres of greenhouses, and an employee roster of 500 workers. In 1924, financial difficulties resulted in C. F. Seabrook losing the company to Del Bay Farms, Inc. He managed to buy back the business in 1929, the same month the stock market crashed, plunging the nation into the Great Depression.

During the Depression, Seabrook ingenuity made the best of a bad situation. Facing a surplus of cabbage, Belford Seabrook turned the crop into sauerkraut, canned it in the company's canning factory (pictured here), and sold it to the state for emergency relief rations. By raising dust bowl cattle from the federal relief program, the company also turned local surplus potatoes and carrots into beef stew for state distribution to needy families.

Leaving nothing to chance, C. F. constructed not one, but two railroad connections alongside the company's storage houses to guarantee competitive shipping rates from the rail lines. One set of tracks linked to the Central Railroad of New Jersey, while the other connected with the Pennsylvania Railroad. In this undated photograph, railroad cars stand ready to roll, stocked with Seabrook produce.

While most farmers relied on weather predictions to guide them, Mother Nature had nothing on Seabrook Farms. The company's climatology laboratory, which was affiliated with Johns Hopkins University, used cutting-edge research to pinpoint, down to the day, when it was most beneficial to plant crops. The laboratory, pictured here during a 1950 open house, developed the planting slide rule, which calculated a vegetable's growth in relation to the climatic calendar.

Pictured here in 1945, Kehler E. Kimmel checks the weather station outside the Seabrook farm office. The weather station was checked regularly for accurate temperature and weather-related data. This information was then provided to the climatology laboratory and other essential departments involved in scheduling planting, watering, fertilizing, and harvesting activities.

A. M. Edgerton (second from left), an Asgrow Seed representative, examines a test plot of sweet corn with research staff members, from left to right, Vernon Ichisaka, Dr. Frank App, Don McAllister, and Jack Seabrook in the 1950s. The research team worked with Asgrow to produce seed varieties best suited to grow quality produce for processing.

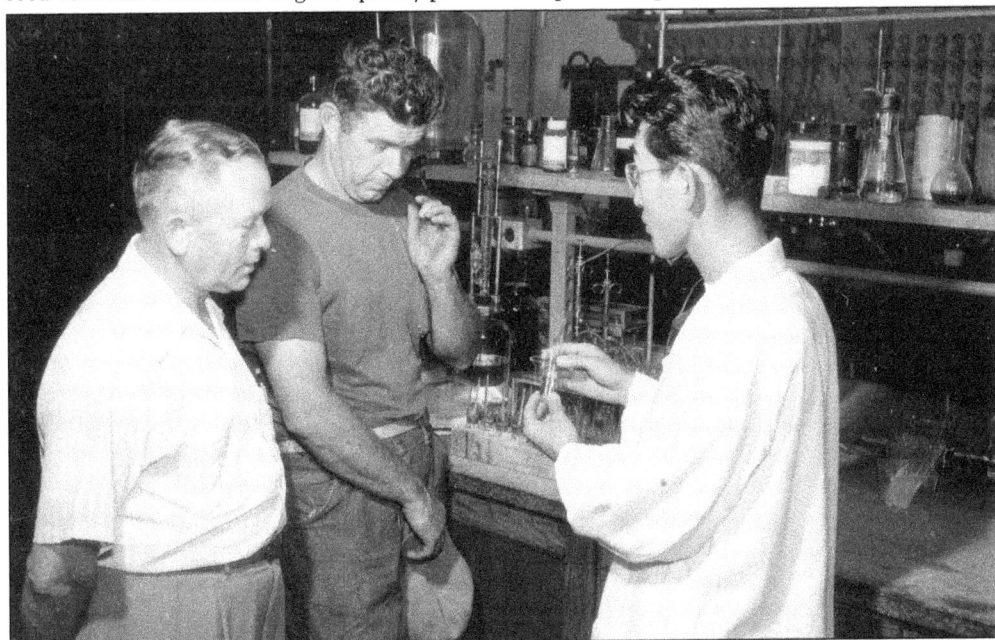

Company chemists in the soil laboratory regularly analyzed the soil temperature and mineral and water content to ensure the soil was properly fertilized before planting began. Tests also were conducted throughout the growing season so the proper nutrients could be kept in the soil at all times. In this October 1952 photograph, John Nakamura performs a typical soil test.

Seabrook's unique farming and processing system left nothing to chance. Quality control laboratory workers like (from left to right) unidentified, John Nakamura, Wako Yokoyama, and Henry Wakai constantly monitored the water treatment system, processing equipment, and final products to ensure consistency.

Irida Mattioli offers a closer look at Seabrook's state-of-the-art equipment in the quality control laboratory.

C. F. Seabrook (right) proudly shows off a portion of his vast operation from atop a Seabrook tractor. At its peak, the company owned 20,000 acres and contracted with area farmers tending 35,000 additional acres in South Jersey, Delaware, Maryland, and Pennsylvania. The Seabrook operation produced 90 million pounds of vegetables and fruit annually, meeting 15 percent of the country's frozen produce needs.

In the mid-1920s, C. F. moved his family, including his wife, Norma; daughter, Thelma; and three sons, into this Polk Lane home in Upper Deerfield. The home's grounds highlighted the elder Seabrook's only real hobby—planning and overseeing magnificent English gardens. The house, which was located in the company's established town center, remained the family home until 1968, when it was converted into Seabrook House, a facility for recovering alcoholics.

At the age of nine, each of C. F. Seabrook's three sons—Belford (as seen on the left of the photograph on the left), Courtney (seen on the right of the photograph on the left), and Jack—was expected to work a full 60-hour week in the fields each summer. By the age of 12, each was handed responsibilities as a gang boss or a foreman. Belford served as foreman during the construction of Seabrook's main artery, Route 77, at the age of 14, and Jack assumed the vital role of produce grader at the young age of 13. At the time of Jack's appointment, C. F. warned his gangly youngest son to "Be careful, your head sticks above the crowd both literally and figuratively, and a lot of people will try to knock it off." Below, from left to right, Belford, Jack, C. F., and Courtney discuss business over lunch in June 1949.

C. F. introduced industrial techniques such as assembly lines and product research into the business of farming. In 1921, B. C. Forbes, future founder of *Fortune* magazine, called him "the Henry Ford of Agriculture." At one point, the Seabrook assembly line process generated two million packages of frozen vegetables and fruit each day.

Seabrook Farms began experimenting with frozen foods in 1913 and became the first company to freeze fruits and vegetables for mass consumption after teaming with Clarence Birdseye in the 1930s. The *New York Times* credited Seabrook Farms with introducing Americans to frozen foods and thereby "helping change the eating habits of the nation." The company's first frozen food experiment involved 20,000 pounds of Seabrook-grown and -processed lima beans, which were frozen in an on-site plant previously used to produce ice for its rail transport cars during World War I. In this photograph, visitors tour the quick-freezing process, which used steam-powered ammonia compressors.

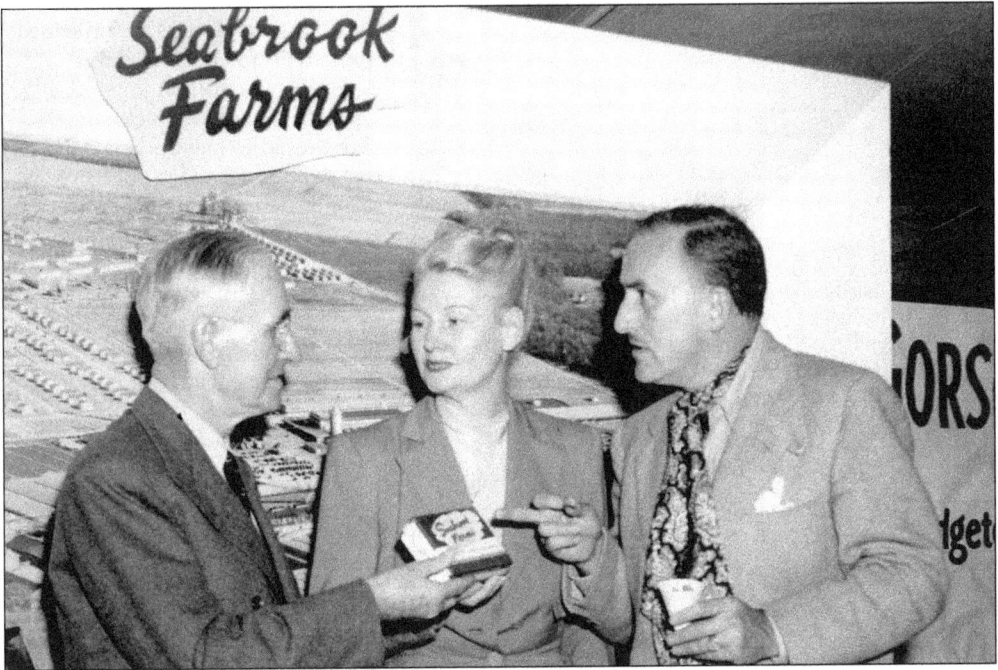

The company began competing with Birdseye and other brands packaged in its plant in 1943, when it introduced the Seabrook Farms label. The brand logo was designed using the signature of C. F. Seabrook himself, seen here (at left) promoting the product at a county fair. Seabrook's brand slogan accurately boasted "We grow our own so we know it's good, and we freeze it right on the spot."

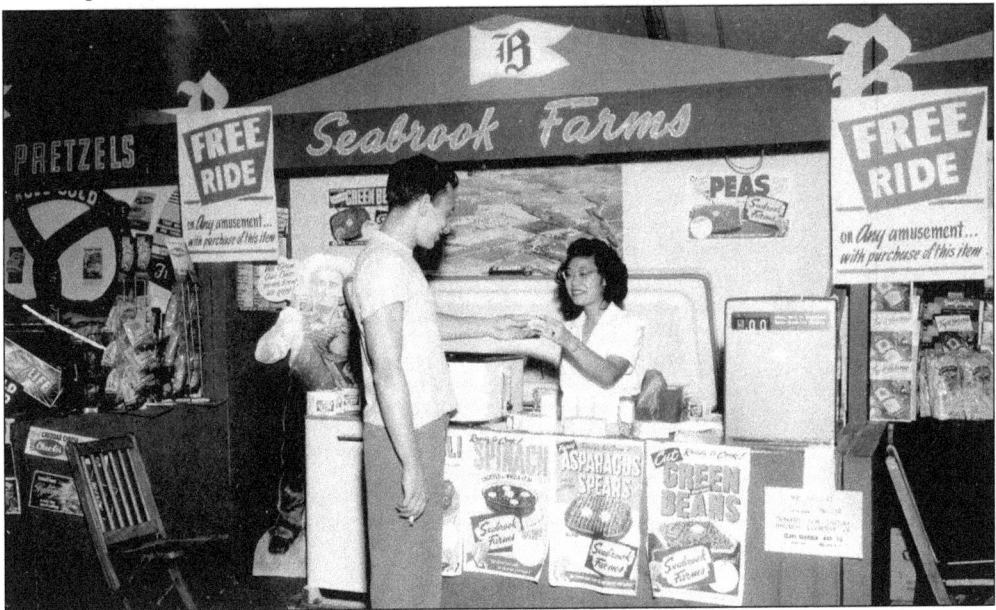

Employee Frances Yamamoto distributes free samples of Seabrook's frozen vegetables to the public at the Cumberland County Fair in September 1950. Personalized marketing was a key component of successful sales, and the company regularly sent workers out to introduce the product to consumers and merchants, especially during the slow winter months.

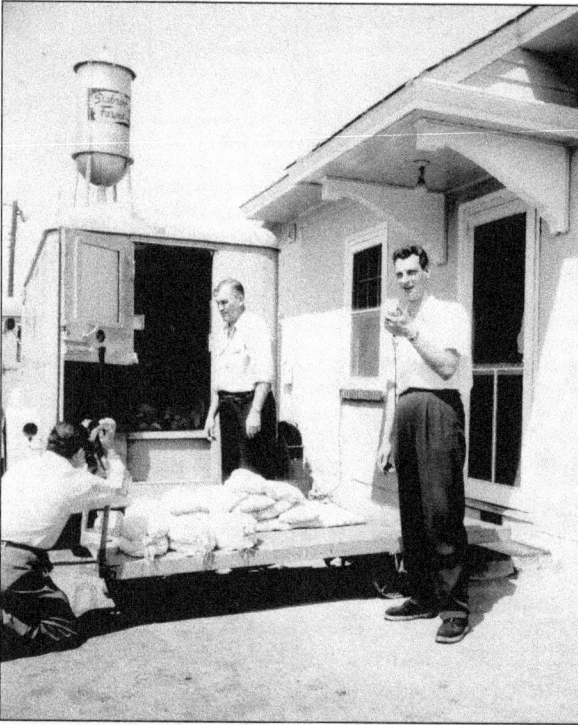

Sacks of silver dollars are unloaded from an armored car to cover Seabrook's payroll on June 30, 1950. Using silver dollars (nicknamed cartwheels) to pay workers during two pay periods was a publicity stunt to demonstrate Seabrook's economic might. On each day, two Brink's trucks hauled in 150 sacks, each containing $1,000 in coins. With over $150,000 in silver dollars on hand, state troopers were brought in as a precaution.

Factory workers line up for their silver dollar salaries on June 30. A total of 3,200 employees participated in the event, dubbed the Cavalcade of Cartwheels. Nellie T. Ross, the U.S. Mint's first female director (pictured in black) was on hand to distribute the coins. As an added bonus, C. F. Seabrook agreed to donate his weight in silver dollars to charity. Weighing 160 pounds, he contributed $2,560 to those in need.

Seabrook Farms took a visionary approach toward fulfilling its constant need for inexpensive labor, reaching out across the country and around the world to families in desperate need of work and the chance to begin a new life. In the 1940s and 1950s, the company employed the most culturally diverse workforce of any rural industrial plant in the United States, including German prisoners of war; refugees from Russia, Italy, Austria, and the Baltic States; and a wide range of island residents. Above, Miiko Sasaki reads to an ethnically diverse group of young children in 1952. Below, Seabrook children participate in a childcare center program.

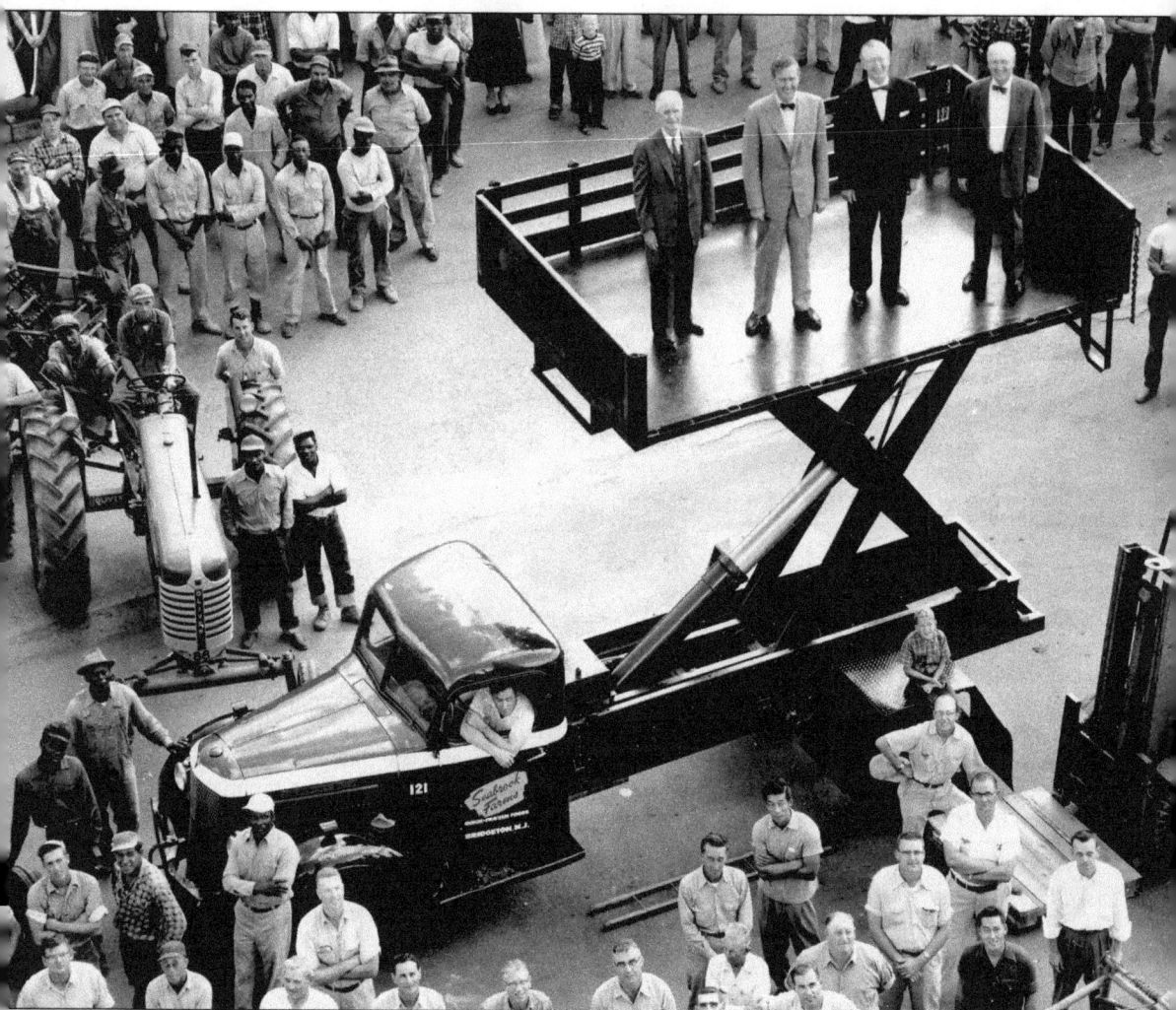

C. F. Seabrook and his sons stand atop a hydraulic lift truck bed surrounded by workers as part of a photo shoot for *Life* magazine on October 14, 1954. The five-page color spread, which ran on January 3, 1955, was titled "Biggest Vegetable Factory on Earth" and irked Seabrook's frozen food competitor General Foods, which frequently paid for similar spreads to market its Birdseye brand in the magazine. When this photograph was taken, C. F. held the position of chairman, Jack was president, Courtney was vice president of marketing, and Belford was vice president of engineering. Scattered in the crowd are Leif "Wolf" Lloyd, Jack "Ogden" Dickerson, Charles Clark, Leonard Brandrup, Charles Hetzell, Jesse Williams, William Hoover, Don McAllister, Chubby Weber Sr., Ben Mixner, John Wallace, Bob Groves, Hoagy Williams, Ken "Jelly" Gondo, Ray Huster, Linwood Munyon, and Willy Nakamaura. A mere four years after the *Life* article appeared, Seabrook Farms closed its doors when C. F. sold his controlling interest in the company to Seeman Brothers, leading his sons to sell as well. Seeman closed the company in 1982.

Two

THE FARM

The Seabrook approach to farming, like the company's approach to most things, was based on science and efficiency. Tending 20,000 acres of farmland, located primarily in South Jersey's Salem and Cumberland Counties, the Seabrook operation left nothing to chance. A barrage of tests was conducted by the company's various on-site laboratories before a single seed was sown, and from planting day to harvest, extensive scientific studies were ongoing.

Farming at Seabrook was business, pure and simple. Company research and unique planting techniques allowed Seabrook Farms to extend the growing season from March through November and increase production across its sprawling farmlands by growing as many as five crops on each plot of land over the course of a single season. Seabrook farming innovation even managed to triumph over the natural rhythm of the day by extending daylight hours using portable floodlights to illuminate up to 10 acres at a time for evening fieldwork.

Crops ranging from apples to wax beans were successfully grown at "the world's biggest vegetable farm," where quantity and quality went hand in hand. Since this dual accomplishment was the result of careful scientific study and agricultural skill, C. F. Seabrook never took the achievement lightly. As he explained in a 1921 issue of *The American Magazine,* "The people who write poems to farming never got up before dawn to milk cows seven days a week and never weeded onions on their knees in the heat and mosquitoes."

A. P. Seabrook was said to have been the first farmer in the area to use a gasoline-powered tractor, a farming advancement that increased efficiency while decreasing manpower needs. In this photograph, a Seabrook worker cultivates one of the company's fields aboard an early tractor.

A fleet of Seabrook tractors rolls out to plow a field in preparation for the planting season in the 1940s or 1950s. As early as 1921, the company was relying heavily on tractors to prepare the soil. In that year, Seabrook owned seven tractors. A mere three years later the fleet's number had jumped to 10.

Migrant workers sow seeds using hand-cranked sowers, working together to thoroughly broadcast seed across the field. In some instances, four or five crops were planted in a single plot over the course of the growing season, with new seeds sown between a nearly mature crop before hand-harvesting took place.

Maintaining proper moisture in the fields was accomplished through a series of moveable overhead irrigation systems, as well as stationary ones. Here Pete Brothers adjusts the pressure on one of Seabrook's field watering systems. Seabrook's high-pressure movable system could broadcast up to two inches of water per acre in less then two hours.

In the early days, cultivating the fields required considerable manpower. In the above photograph, field laborers tend to a spinach crop. Below, a cabbage field is cultivated using a plow and field mule in the 1930s.

In 1913, Seabrook constructed its first large greenhouse to jump-start the growing season. This 1919 aerial view of several of the early greenhouses, each measuring 300 feet long by 60 feet wide, also shows the company's main office and power plant, and several Seabrook homes. At the time, Seabrook Farms's Upper Deerfield property maintained nine boardinghouses for single men from Philadelphia and the surrounding areas who were seasonally employed.

Seabrook's network of greenhouses was known for nurturing quality seedlings. In this photograph, one side of a greenhouse is being prepared for new cuttings, while the other contains seedlings ready to be transplanted.

In addition to raising seedlings for field planting, some of Seabrook's greenhouses were used to grow early crops to maturity. In this photograph, hothouse lettuce is carefully harvested by migrant workers.

In the fields, crops were tended to with the same care as the greenhouse seedlings. In this photograph, fertilizer is being broadcast across Seabrook's crops. The timing and chemical composition of each application was based on careful laboratory testing to determine the mineral content of the soil and the overall health of the plants.

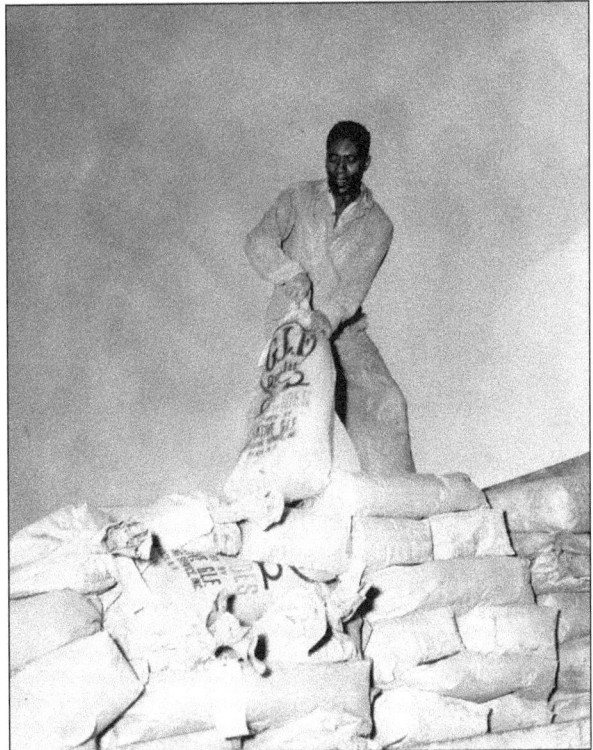

Pests had to be controlled as well, a daunting task considering Seabrook's large-scale operation. Here a worker hefts sacks of insecticide in preparation for the ongoing battle against bugs and disease.

31

While most farms contracted with crop-dusting companies that flew up and down the East Coast following the growing season, Seabrook Farms maintained its own fleet of crop-dusting planes. In this photograph, Jack Seabrook (left) reviews an aerial map as one of the company's planes prepares for takeoff.

In later years, when the company's crop-dusting fleet was modernized, helicopters were outfitted for the task to take the place of the traditional crop-dusting planes. In this photograph, pesticides are loaded into a Seabrook helicopter.

Seabrook's crops were inspected regularly during the growing season as well as at harvest time. In this photograph, supervisor William Hoover inspects cauliflower heads as laborers handpick the crop in the Upper Deerfield fields.

Belford Seabrook (right) inspects lima bean plants during the harvest.

Field-workers spent long days stooped in the fields weeding around delicate plants to ensure the crops were not choked out by the rapidly growing vegetation. Here workers tend to a spinach field.

Vernon Ichisaka weighs baskets of beans as they are harvested in the field.

Iceberg lettuce is harvested and crated at Seabrook Farms during World War II. The overhead irrigation system visible in the background is an early moveable Seabrook system.

Field-workers dressed against the brisk weather pose among the plentiful crook-necked squash crop during the fall harvest season.

Bushel baskets of freshly picked apples are set along the roadside for collection in the photograph above. Below, a truck is loaded with apples for transport to the processing plant, where they will be turned into apple juice. Anticipating the repeal of Prohibition, Seabrook built a distillery in 1934 to convert its excess apples into brandy. When the 21st Amendment to the Constitution became law in April of that year, Seabrook Farms was issued the first liquor-manufacturing license.

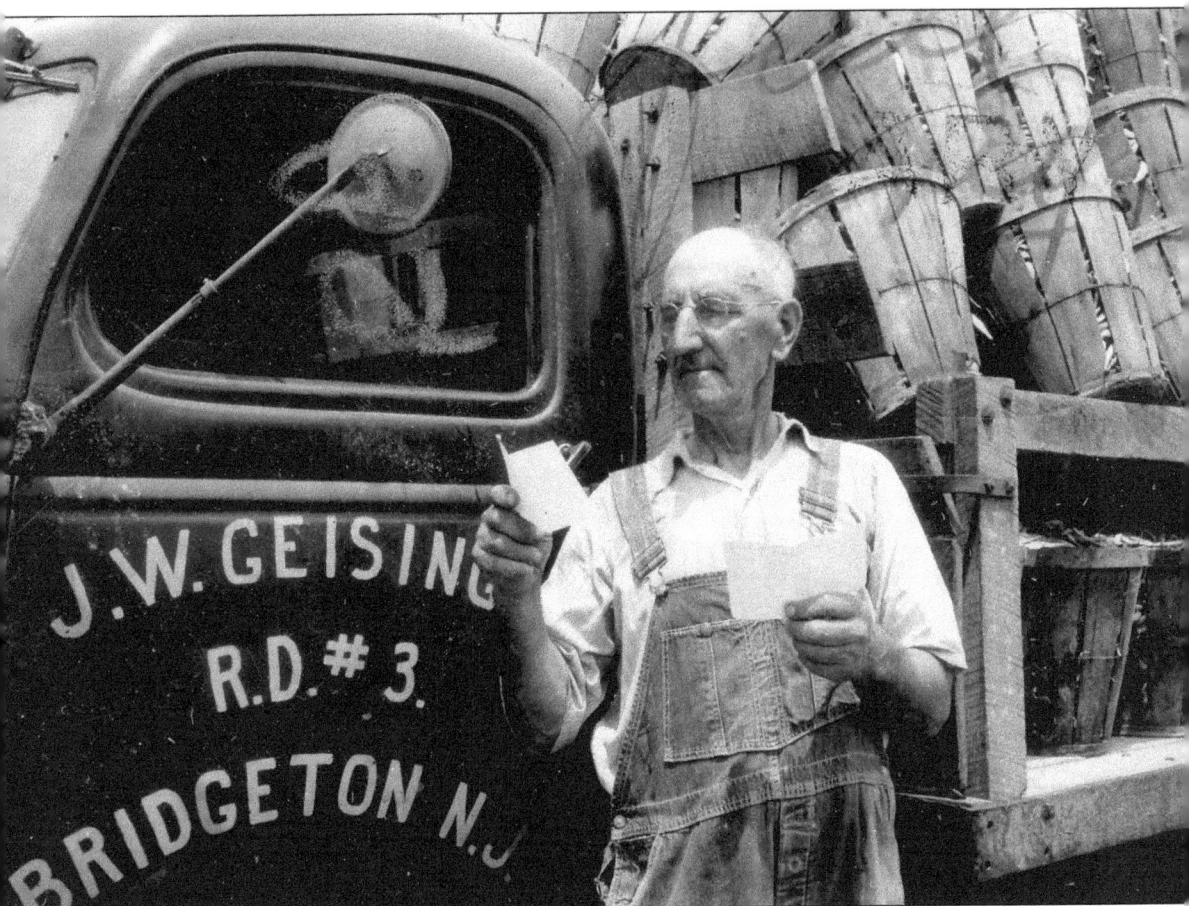

In addition to its 20,000 acres of corporate-held farmland, Seabrook worked with regional farmers to supply additional crops for its processing operation. This Bridgeton farmer, one of 1,169 contract farmers in South Jersey, Delaware, Maryland, and Pennsylvania providing the company with produce from a total of 35,000 additional acres, delivers green beans to the plant in July 1952.

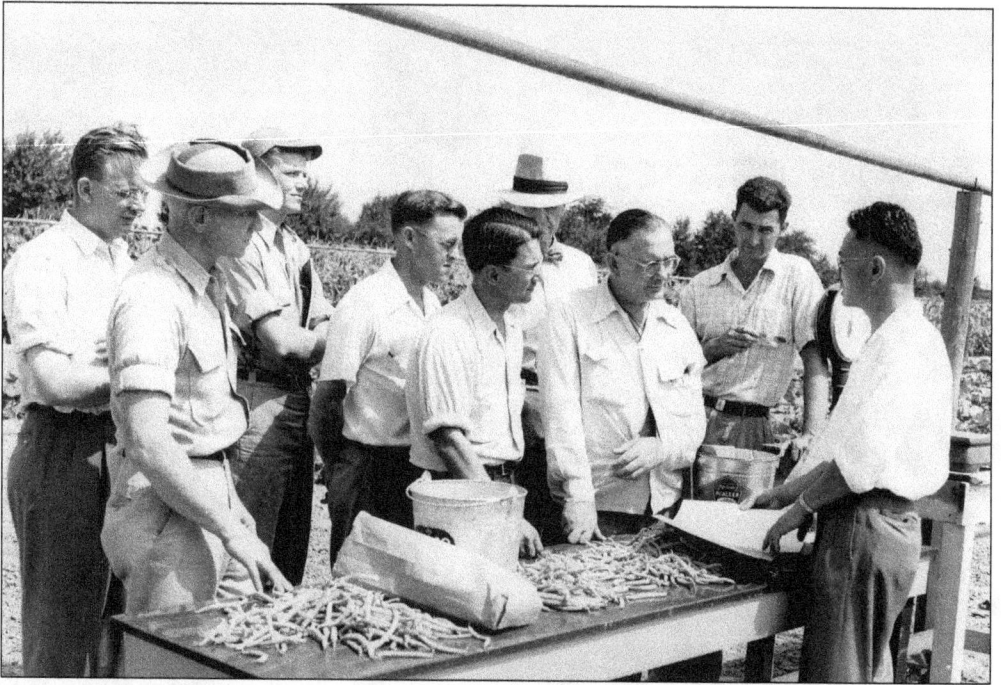

Vernon Ichisaka (right) demonstrates bean-sorting procedures in the field at Seabrook, using freshly harvested green beans. Hand-harvested beans were gathered in baskets weighing approximately 23 pounds each.

Field laborers hand-harvest spinach, which was both the first and the last crop picked at Seabrook each year. Spinach was first picked in late March. It closed out the growing season with a November harvest.

In later years, spinach and several other crops were harvested using automated machines like the one pictured below, which marched through the fields gathering crops. Several different mechanized harvesters where employed at Seabrook, designed specifically for the type of crop being picked. These mechanized harvesters ran so smoothly that portable lights were set up in the fields so work could continue through the night during prime picking season. In the photograph above, an automatic harvester gets a close inspection by Seabrook personnel.

Planks for Seabrook crop crates were cut from whole logs at the company's sawmill. Here box shop workers assemble crates in the field in anticipation of the latest crop being harvested.

A Seabrook Farms truck hauls crates of freshly picked peas to the factory for processing.

Three

THE FACTORY

Seabrook's sprawling factory operation hummed around the clock during the lengthy growing season, processing close to three dozen different varieties of fruits and vegetables under more than a dozen different labels. In fact, demand for produce to feed the plant was so great that along with the company's substantial yield from its own 20,000 acres, Seabrook contracted with farmers around South Jersey, as well as Delaware, Maryland, and Pennsylvania, to generate produce on an additional 35,000 acres.

While the Birdseye frozen food contract was the catalyst that turned Seabrook Farms's canning and packaging operation into a food-processing giant, once that innovative product hit the market, a steady stream of product labels began pouring from the factory. In time, while Birdseye went out on its own, Seabrook Farms earned a reputation for quality under its own label. Later, in 1957, the company purchased the vegetable lines of two other big names in frozen foods at the time—SnowCrop and Minute Maid.

As the first agricultural operation to use industrial processes such as assembly lines, the Seabrook plant included facilities to clean, sort, blanch, and freeze (or can in some instances) massive quantities of produce. While machines made processing faster, it did nothing to reduce the long hours of repetitive labor demanded of Seabrook factory workers who shoveled produce into vast viners, hunched over sorting lines, and kept the packaging lines moving during their 12-hour shifts.

Seabrook's factory operation included seven separate processing systems, each designed to handle specific produce. At its peak, nearly two million packages a day were processed at Seabrook's 23-acre plant, which was capable of handling 33 different products. The plant and its front platform are seen here in winter.

Once specially designed corn harvesters rolled through the fields, stripping the ears off the stalks and dropping the stalks to the ground to be used as fodder, the ears were hauled by panel truck and dumped into the elevator shaft using a portable hitch like this one to lift the truck's front end.

A load of corn is hand-shoveled into the plant's husking machine in 1952, after harvesting.

Migrant workers armed with long-handled pitchforks feed harvested pea plants into the automatic viners, which separate the vines from the pods, slit open the pods, extract the peas, and chop up the vines for use as fertilizer in the fields. This strenuous work was later handled by machines.

Crews like this worked from dawn to dusk in the summer heat pitching materials into the towering viners. Shortly after World War I, Seabrook provided work for over 100 men believed to have been soldiers in the White Russian Army, which was defeated in the Russian Revolution. Many of them worked at Seabrook's viner stations, finding the labor a welcome alternative to the labor camps or death sentences awaiting them at home.

A worker monitors peas as he fills boxes at the viner station.

Peas are unloaded from a field truck onto the front platform for weighing in, the first step of processing.

Richard Nishimura prepares to read the scale as overflowing crates are unloaded onto the platform.

Once weighed, raw peas are transported via these towering elevators to the third floor of Seabrook's massive factory for processing. In the 1950s, the company's pea and lima bean processing facility was the largest of its kind in the world.

Workers like Steve Linkachuck (left) and Flavio Butler (right) check hoppers full of peas before they begin the two-and-a-half-hour trek through the plant for washing, blanching, sorting, packaging, and freezing.

Peas pass through water sprays for a thorough washing before being reboxed and sent on to the blanching machines.

47

Steam heat is used in the blanching process to sterilize the peas. They then float through a briny bath designed to separate the tender young peas from the more mature ones. Here blanched peas are added to the brine and begin their journey to the appropriate sorting lines.

Approximately 600 cartons of peas were filled every minute on the Marathon pea line around 1950. At right, Hisano Tazumi (foreground) and Julie Nicosa prepare cartons for filling. Once filled, underweight cartons were booted from the line (as seen at the left in the photograph above) and good cartons made their way to the wrapping machine to be packaged under the Birdseye, SnowCrop, Seabrook, and more than a dozen lesser-known labels. Seabrook's packaging operation was originally called the Deerfield Packing Corporation.

Waxed paper overwrapping is added to each package to prevent moisture loss in the soon-to-be-frozen produce. Here a worker feeds wrappers into a machine that will carefully and quickly package each carton.

Shuichi Yoshizaki (left) and Frances Kawajiri Minato (right) transfer wrapped cartons from the wrapping machine line to the freezer line.

Ed Dorsey loads Seabrook-grown and -processed vegetables into the freezer for quick freezing at minus 37 degrees. Cartons are frozen block-hard in two hours.

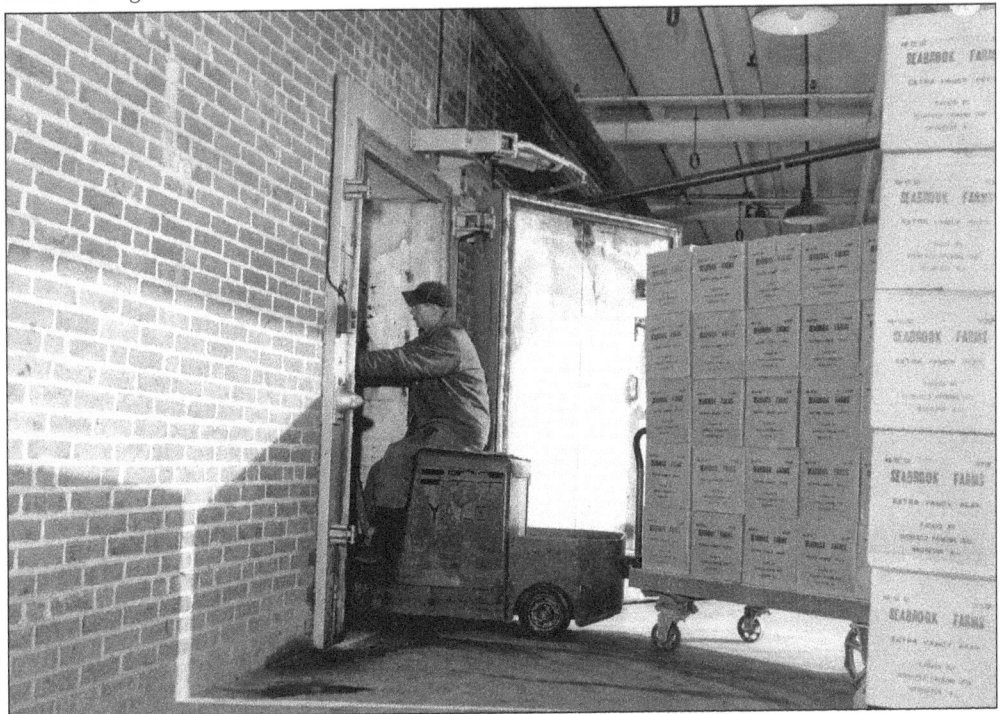

Frozen produce makes its way into Seabrook's cold storage warehouse, operated by the company under the name of the Cumberland Warehouse Corporation.

Cases of frozen produce head for temporary housing in the sub-zero warehouse, which could store up to 50 million cartons for future shipment to distributors.

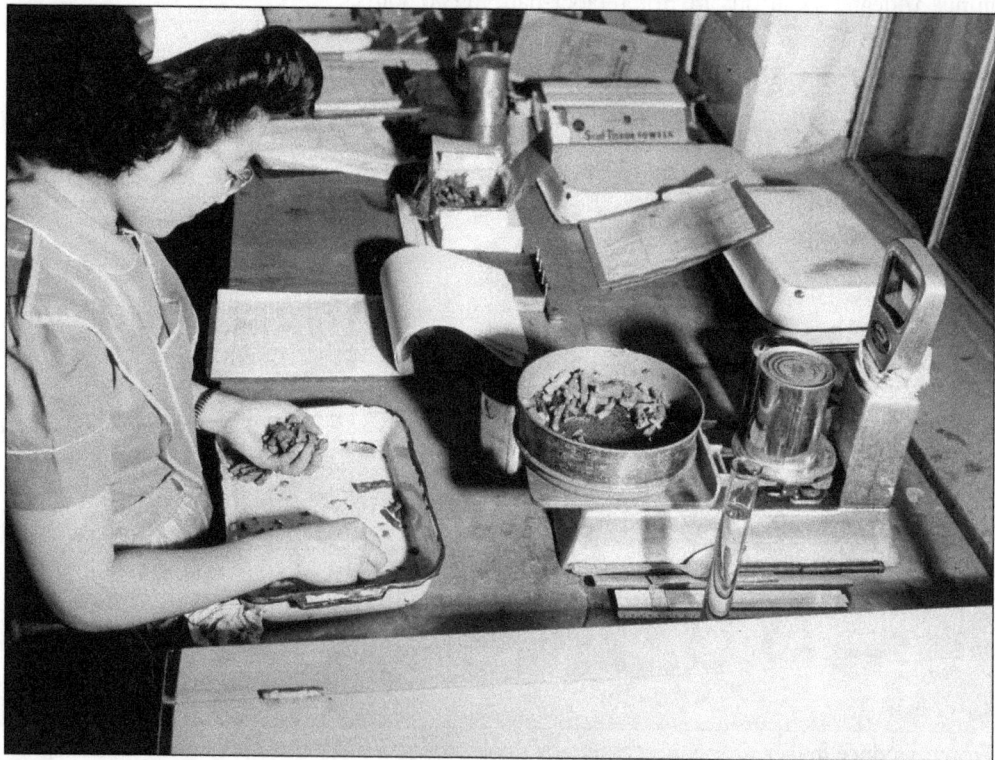
Helen Bano grades asparagus in the quality control department.

The world's largest quick-freezer, Seabrook's freezing system utilized Frick compressors. The two-stage freezing system employed compressors like the ones pictured here, as well as condensers, brine coolers, and room piping. On windless nights, the ammonia fumes generated by the compressors filled the air. Seabrook's impressive compressor needs kept the Frick factory in Pennsylvania from shutting down during the Depression.

Whenever possible, Seabrook preferred to use women on its sorting lines rather than men, finding that the repetitive work often frustrated men who were assigned to work the lines and that women adapted better to the quick pace. Here Katie Schmidt processes spinach on the sorting line.

Carolyn Davis quickly cuts off defects from beets as they make their way down the line. Seabrook's beets were canned in the company's canning plant.

During all but the winter months, factory staff worked 12-hour shifts, with a day off every two weeks when they switched shifts. The company offered no paid holidays or sick time. In this photograph, workers head home after a hard day on September 3, 1952. The time would be shortly after 6:00 a.m. or 6:00 p.m., which were the regularly scheduled times for shift changes.

Workers dressed in their Seabrook blue uniforms and starched white caps line up at the paymaster's station to collect their wages at the end of the week. Typical of the day, women earned 5¢ an hour less than men.

Four

BEHIND THE SCENES

While the farm and factory operations brought Seabrook Farms fame and fortune, it was the behind-the-scenes support network—from office staff and laboratory technicians to blacksmiths and engine room personnel—that kept things running smoothly. With such a sizeable support network, communication was key, and the Seabrook company, even with its cultural diversity, made the task seem easy, holding regular staff meetings, employing bilingual supervisors, and publishing a multi-language company newsletter called, appropriately enough, the *Seabrooker*.

Expectations for new employees were clearly spelled out in the *Seabrooker* by C. F. himself, "No sulkers or people with touchy feelings need apply. Anyone who says that he can get a job from 'so and so' any time he wants had better take it . . . Our regular workday is a ten-hour day. However, the work consists in doing whatever the employer feels like asking at any minute of the day or night. Anyone who can meet the above specifications we invite to join our growing organization, which still has room not only at the top, but at the bottom, and halfway up as well."

For those willing to follow the Seabrook guidelines for employment, security was virtually guaranteed. Company policy dictated that in each family, one adult would be promised full-time employment and the other would be guaranteed at least seasonal work. Medical benefits also were provided, along with company housing, and meals and supplies were temporarily free for newcomers struggling to settle in.

The main office, located on Parsonage Road near the company fire department, was the hub of Seabrook's operations. The main floor housed both C. F. Seabrook's and Jack Seabrook's offices and support staff, the receptionist, and the treasury department. Accounting filled the second floor, while the credit department was housed in the basement. The main office annex was constructed later to accommodate the sales staff and an early computer department.

During the growing season, Seabrook's corps of operators, including June Yoshioka, pictured here, manned the main office phones 24 hours a day, relaying updates from mobile field units to in-house supervisors.

Keeping track of the vast farm and factory operations' staffing needs required considerable organization, especially when Seabrook was called upon to produce 60 million pounds of processed vegetables and fruit under a government contract during World War II. This bulletin board in the personnel/scheduling department tracked staffing to ensure around-the-clock coverage when needed.

Personnel department workers prepare to file a stack of paperwork on new hires. At its peak employment in 1947, Seabrook retained close to 5,000 workers whose differing backgrounds often required bilingual interpreters. The language and cultural differences, as well as the massive size of the workforce, required meticulous paperwork on each employee to ensure smooth operations.

Here a newcomer, identified only as Alice, holds her badge number in place as personnel department employee Loretta Romanda prepares to take her photograph for her employee identification badge.

Even with their heavy workload, Seabrook's farm office staff members found time to celebrate special occasions like Bob Miller's birthday. Celebrating with Miller, who supervised the migrant worker recruiting, are (from left to right) Peg Miller, Pearl Minch, Betty Gaunt, Lisa Levi, and June Yoshioka.

The billing department handled $25 million in gross receipts in 1954 alone. Pictured here in the early 1950s are members of the billing staff, including Ruth Matsumoto, Paul Powers, Florence Charleston, Toshi Hashimoto, and Maris Kart.

Communication between Seabrook's various operations often required sharing paperwork between departments spread throughout the company's sprawling campus. This cart may have been the intercompany mail truck.

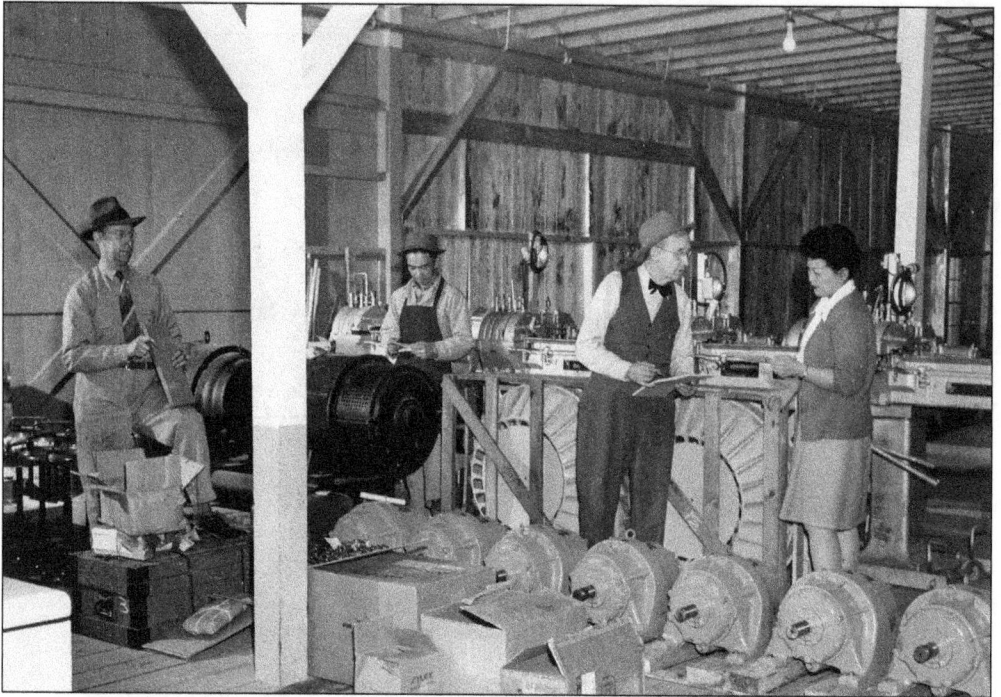

Keeping track of everything from dry goods to machine parts was the task of Seabrook's receiving and supply department. Here supplies are checked in with a secretary in the receiving and supply department.

Dry goods warehouse personnel take a moment to pose for a photograph. The warehouse primarily stocked 10-ounce and institutional-sized cartons for produce packing, a wide range of labels denoting the product and specific distributor's name and logo, and collapsible cardboard shipping boxes.

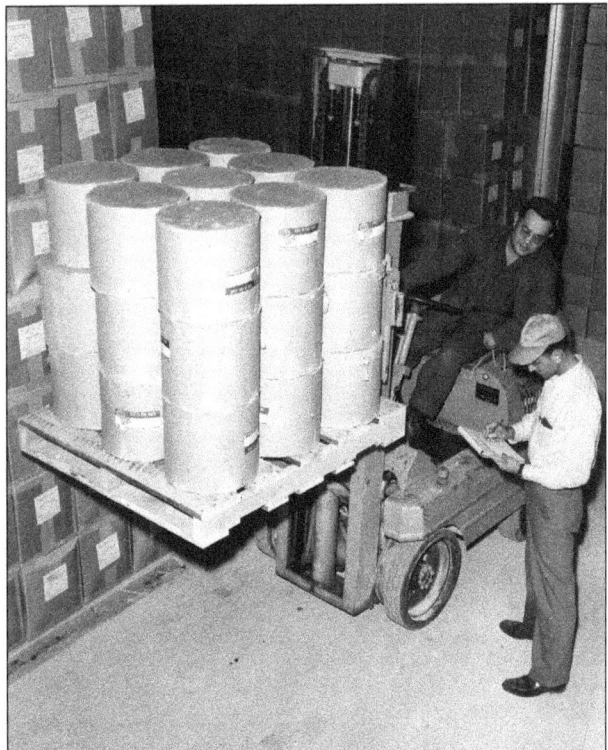

Paper rolls for the wrapping machine are inventoried by Jim Omura in the dry goods warehouse.

Running a smooth operation required regular staff meetings like this plant supervisors meeting. Those in attendance include Gladys Carter, Virginia Forren, Margaret Yoshida, Chickie Furushima, Vera Aoki, Alice Matsui, Louise Smith, Stella Messick, Ichiyo Nakai, Frank Hemingway, John Ferrillo, Albert Vilms, Lynn Maxey, Edna Beal, John Melchiorre, John Fuyuume, Asta Riivald, and Asta Sheppard.

Jack Seabrook gives a report to his staff, including Virginia Forren, Lucille Hayes, Fitch Maxson, Bernard Steppe, Lee Towsen, Bob Miller, Richard Nishimura, Jack Marone, Charles Nagao, Gene Sakamoto, Chickie Furushima, Rose Sakamoto, Victor Cubberly, and Harold Emerson.

Factory workers were required to punch in and out each day at one of Seabrook's time clocks, which were installed throughout the plant. Time cards were distributed at the front gate as employees arrived for their shift and collected at the time clock stations at the end of each shift.

Scientific research played a significant role in Seabrook's success, and each field of research had its own laboratory. In this undated photograph, Fusa Wadamoto works on an experiment in the climatology laboratory.

John Nakamura checks on a test being conducted in the soil laboratory by an unidentified technician in December 1949.

Kaz Kobayashi conducts a test on just-picked peas in the quality control department. Tests in this laboratory often involved the Seabrook-developed tenderometer, which was used to determine the tenderness of a crop as part of the company's harvesting index.

The effectiveness of crop dusting depended to a great extent on calculating the degree of air turbulence, so at Seabrook the turbulence level was carefully measured before sending planes up to spray. The device shown here detonated a small charge of powder, and the amount of time it took to disperse was used to calculate if weather conditions were favorable for dusting.

Engine room workers install a new compressor in January 1951. In the early days, the engine room was staffed with four men per eight-hour shift. Chief engineers in Seabrook's history included Tom Martin, Herb Seibert, and James Donnelly. Other engine room employees included Robert Smith, Primo Bushardo, Bob Ford, Don Bonch, Richard Hanny, Bruce Clark, and Wilburn Jenkins.

Built at the end of World War II, the factory's steam plant met the company's steam needs for blanching vegetables and for sanitizing and cleaning equipment. Tom Martin served as chief engineer at the steam plant, and Clarence Trull, Jim Ford, Arthur Griffith, and John Hoffman shared eight-hour two-man shifts.

Supervisor John Shaw (right) provides instruction to crew members in the blacksmith shop. The smell of coal smoke and burning hooves filled the air around the shop, where four forges glowed almost constantly to keep up with Seabrook's needs.

Jim Cox is dwarfed by a portion of Seabrook's electric power plant during one of his regular inspections.

A bit of winter training from the Caterpillar Company turned former farm laborers like Jack Dickerson (right) into repairmen, allowing them to maintain Seabrook's field equipment in the company's own repair shop rather than paying for outside service.

Keeping Seabrook's fleet of trucks and cars up and running required a skilled crew of mechanics working full time in the garage. Mechanics pictured here include Tom Kazaoko (second row, wearing the light overalls and hat with badge) and David Link (first row, first man kneeling on left). Garage work was one of the only chores for permanent workers who were housed at Seabrook year round.

Garage workers take time out for ice cream and cake, most likely to celebrate a birthday. The workload escalated annually for Seabrook's mechanics. Between 1921 and 1924, the company's stable of animals dropped from 300 horses and mules to 100, and the fleet of trucks and cars rose from about 10 to approximately 40.

Seabrook's fleet of trucks stands ready for inspection. The company's Cumberland Auto and Truck division was located at 41 Atlantic Street in Bridgeton.

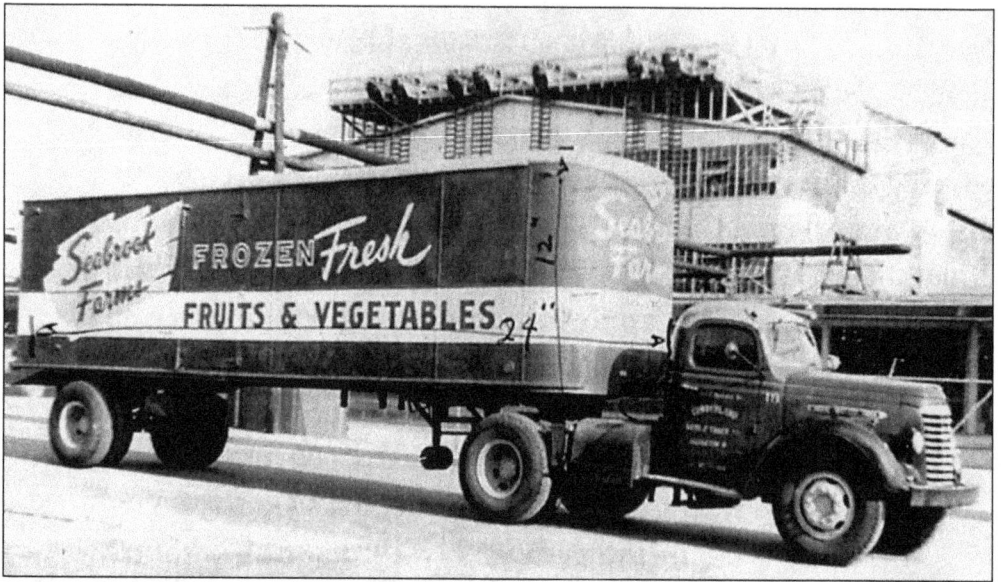

Early refrigeration trucks like this one, loaded with frozen Seabrook produce, were a common sight on the nation's highways in the 1950s. The tractor-trailers' refrigeration systems, designed by Belford Seabrook, were powered by a dual-volt motor, providing 24 volts of power while on the road and 110 volts when parked in a warehouse. Seabrook regularly shipped to states east of the Mississippi River.

One of Seabrook's trucks unloads a plane full of peas flown from a western Pennsylvania farm for transport to the factory for processing.

In just eight years, C. F. Seabrook's engineering corporation built the infrastructure needed for his massive factory operation: 35 miles of roads; power plants; cold storage facilities; two railroad lines to connect with nearby commercial lines; dams; various workshops and garages; a wide swath of housing settlements for employees; and pumping stations and the sewage treatment plant under construction here. German prisoners of war, part of Hitler's famed Deutsches Afrika Korps (DAK), were housed in a nearby abandoned Civilian Conservation Corps camp and dug the ditches needed to lay water pipes at Seabrook.

After 1934, production was so high at Seabrook that construction projects, like this factory addition underway in March 1953, proceeded year round, and expansion continued virtually nonstop for nearly 20 years. More than 100 construction workers were on Seabrook's payroll at that time, with only steelworkers and bricklayers hired as outside contractors. Among those regularly contracted to work on Seabrook construction projects was the company owned and operated by bricklayer John B. "Jack" Kelly, father of Grace Kelly, a friend of the Seabrook family.

Five

A CULTURAL
MELTING POT

Seabrook Farms's seemingly insatiable need for farm and factory workers drew able-bodied laborers from the four corners of the country as well as both hemispheres, all eager to work hard for low wages and the chance to begin a new life. Although they hailed from more than 25 nations and spoke over 30 different languages and dialects, this diverse population worked side by side in harmony, in keeping with the company's strict policy of nondiscrimination.

Word of Seabrook's opportunities originally spread by word of mouth, from regional Italians who labored in the fields one summer to their relatives in war-ravaged Italy, and knowledgeable immigration agents who directed new arrivals to the company's doors. Later C. F. Seabrook and others made recruiting trips overseas in search of workers and collaborated with the federal government to secure relocation arrangements for Japanese workers who had been placed in internment camps during World War II.

To help them integrate into their new lives, the company sponsored English classes; employed bilingual supervisors; and published its employee newsletter in a variety of languages, including English, Spanish, Japanese, and Estonian. While their backgrounds varied widely, the men, women, and children who came to live and labor at Seabrook Farms built a remarkable community together. Settling in their own little ethnic enclaves allowed them the opportunity to maintain their treasured traditions, including grocery stores stocking their own favorite foods, while working together and gathering for community-wide company events helped them establish new identities as "Seabrookers."

C. F. Seabrook built separate villages for many of the nationalities employed by the company, where people could speak their native languages, eat their native foods, and follow their treasured cultural traditions. The Italian village, pictured here, was the first to be constructed as Italian families began making their way to Seabrook before the start of World War I. Here traditional religious processions were held on saints' days and bread was baked daily in the village's communal brick beehive ovens.

Migrant workers from Southern states line up to apply for work at Seabrook. Large numbers of southern workers began arriving at the company's doors looking for work at the beginning of the Depression. By the early 1940s, as many as 200 men, women, and children from the southern states, many from Appalachia, had made their way to Seabrook in their battered old cars and trucks.

Children use asparagus boxes as tables and chairs during lunch at Orchard Center, one of Seabrook's migrant workers' housing settlements.

Discussions between Philadelphia Quakers and Jack Seabrook led the company to reach out to the Japanese in internment camps during World War II at the same time internees at several camps were looking into Seabrook. With a government allocation of $25 each, and a one-way ticket east, a stream of 2,500 displaced Japanese made their way to Seabrook between 1944 and 1946. Among the early arrivals pictured here are Ellen Nakamura and Fuju Sasaki. An article in a 1944 *Reader's Digest* brought Seabrook Farms to the attention of George Sakamoto, one of the thousands of Japanese Americans held in West Coast internment camps during World War II.

By 1947, Seabrook's residential population boasted the highest concentration of Japanese Americans in the United States, with over 2,500 living at Seabrook. They also represented the largest ethnic group to work for a single U.S. employer at the time. Above, Japanese children at Seabrook salute the American flag in 1945, as World War II rages on.

Talent shows held at Seabrook's community house and the village school always drew crowds of residents, who enjoyed the exposure to various cultural traditions shared during performances, from an Italian song to a dance in wooden shoes by immigrants from Holland. Here Japanese dancers perform at a Seabrook School talent show on March 30, 1952.

From left to right, Jeffery Taniguchi, Karen Takata, Louise Ogata, Ken Ogata, and Michael Asada dress in traditional costume to celebrate the altar, or *onaijin*, handcrafted by Kiyoshi Ohara for the Seabrook Buddhist Church in 1957.

In 1948, the local chapter of the Japanese American Citizens League and American Legion Post 95 in Bridgeton began offering citizenship classes at Seabrook's community house. Headed by Mrs. Herbert Brauer (pictured here helping a potential new citizen study), the program was launched four years before the federal government approved legislation that would allow the Japanese to seek citizenship.

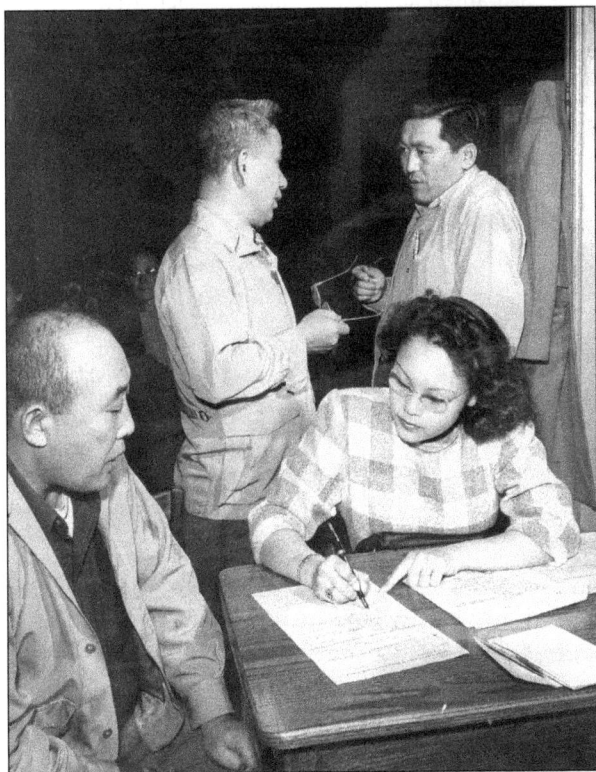

Tats Hasegawa (seated) helps a Japanese worker register for naturalization, as Fuju Sasaki and George Sakamoto confer in the background. On June 29, 1953, just a year after citizenship was available to them, 126 Japanese Americans were naturalized at a ceremony at the Seabrook School. At the time it was the largest group of a single nationality to receive citizenship in one location.

Refugees from war-torn Europe made their way to Seabrook as well, arriving as displaced persons following World War II. Coming from Estonia, Latvia, Lithuania, Poland, Germany, and a number of other nations, they were aided in their efforts to acclimate to their new homes and gain citizenship by members of the recently naturalized Japanese community. Here Keigo Inouye helps European workers complete citizenship papers.

Seabrook's large Estonian population began arriving in 1949 from German refugee camps, where they found themselves as a result of the 1944 Soviet invasion of their homeland. In this photograph, Jack Seabrook (right) and Rev. Hebert Dick (left), of St. John's Lutheran Church, welcome Rahaleid Kaask, the head of Seabrook's first Estonian family. Eventually totaling over 600 men, women, and children, Seabrook's Estonian workers were hired as vegetable and frozen food processors.

Although Estonian refugees told Seabrook recruiters they had farming experience in order to secure jobs, many, in fact, were actually college educated and had held professional jobs in their homeland. Because of their educational backgrounds, they often ended up in supervisory roles. Here Charles Richter (left) registers Estonian teenagers Vallo Truumes and Herbert Schenk for work at Seabrook.

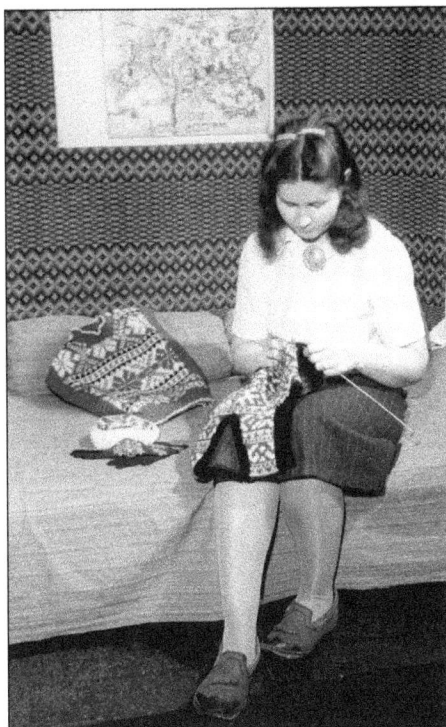

Although Seabrook's residents did assimilate well into American culture, within their small communities traditions remained strong. Here Elsbeth Kiik knits a traditional Estonian-patterned woolen sweater.

Estonian refugees perform a traditional dance at a talent show in March 1952 at the Seabrook School. Occasionally a group would include a friend in a performance, teaching, for example, a Jamaican immigrant to polka and join in for the evening.

Hundreds of West Indies men began arriving at Seabrook around 1941, mostly from Jamaica, Barbados, the Bahamas, and Trinidad. Most were single or left their families behind, as instructed by the company, and many arrived with little more than a change of clothes. In this photograph several Jamaican workers enjoy a game of cricket on their off hours at the Seabrook School playground. The company's apartments can be seen in the background. Jamaican workers, along with residents from Puerto Rico and other parts of the Caribbean, came to Seabrook as contract farmers.

Ultimately three races and more than 25 nationalities worked and lived together at Seabrook in the first half of the 20th century. This photograph of three Seabrook Girl Scouts was taken around 1950.

Six

COMMUNITY LIFE

Time spent at Seabrook Farms, whether as a temporary migrant worker or a permanent employee, was time spent making new friends and experiencing new cultures. Laboring in the fields, factory, and behind-the-scenes operations involved long hours, whether harvesting potatoes, grading asparagus, or processing payroll. But as hard as they worked, the Seabrook settlement was designed so employees could play hard too. To ensure community harmony, C. F. Seabrook himself periodically held meetings with workers to hear complaints and requests concerning housing, working conditions, hours and pay, educational needs, and even where the general store was lacking in ethnic food inventories.

Seabrook children attended the childcare center or the company's school; enjoyed summer day camps and outings; and gathered for scout meetings, team sports, and cultural celebrations. Adults established their own churches; joined social clubs; founded chapters of ethnic organizations like Freedom Lodge 3106 (the Seabrook chapter of the Polish National Alliance); competed on teams like the predominately German Seabrook Soccer Club, which took part in the National Amateur Cup eliminations in 1959; and attended dinners and parties at the community house or in each other's homes.

For many of those who spent time at Seabrook it was home in a way that their most recent residence was not, and each of them made it their own by combining their personal backgrounds with the rural spirit of Seabrook Farms.

From 1943 through 1946, Seabrook Farms recruited African American college girls from the Deep South for summer work. Here a group of girls settle into their apartment at Seabrook. The company flew the girls on a chartered military plane from Atlanta, Georgia, to Philadelphia along with their chaperones and picked them up at the airport in the Seabrook bus.

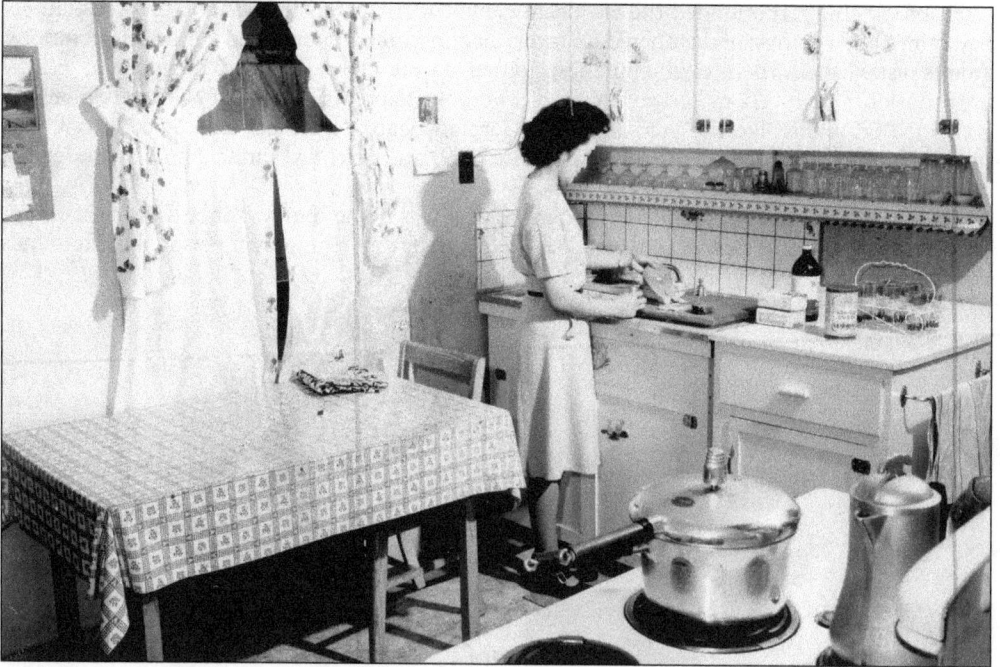

Seabrook's apartments boasted all of the modern kitchen conveniences, as can be seen in this undated photograph.

Single male seasonal and migrant workers lived in 16-foot-by-16-foot prefabricated barracks or "hutments" in Seabrook's Gelston Village. The encampment included centralized bathroom facilities, and meals were served at a central location. This undated photograph shows damage to the structures following a tornado.

Construction is underway at Seabrook's West Village, which provided single-family housing for permanent workers. Located off Route 77, the settlement consisted of First, Second, Third, and Fourth Streets. Permanent housing costs at Seabrook ranged from $4 to $17 a month, depending on the location and size of the residence.

Completed in 1947, West Village homes on First and Second Streets were three-room bungalows with large living rooms and dining areas, as well as full basements.

Children watch the construction of the Gunnison Village portion of West Village in 1953. Gunnison Village homes were located on Third and Fourth Streets and were built on concrete slabs, thus lacking the basements available in the remaining portion of the settlement.

Here is the dining area of one of the bungalows in newly constructed Gunnison Village.

This image displays the living room of a Gunnison Village bungalow.

Seabrook often acquired existing farmhouses as the company purchased farmland. Houses like these were then rented out to select employees at the discretion of the company's housing department.

Beginning in 1944, well before childcare centers were common practice, young children of households where both parents worked spent the day at the Seabrook Child Care Center (also known as the Seabrook Nursery School). The center was funded through the Migrant Division of the State Department of Labor and was open from 7:30 a.m. to 6:00 p.m. Headed by Nillita Fithian and Dorothy Ewell, the school was well staffed by Alice Okino, Marion Umemoto, Mary Yagura, Irene Nakano, Pearline Goldsboro, Margaret Roberts, Marion Lupton, Yoshimitsu Honda, Jessie Stanley, Gertrude Yoshihara, and Shizuo Honda.

Activities at the center included both indoor and outdoor play. Here boys work together to build a fort. Among those pictured are Chuck Koyanagi, Edwin Inouye (with glasses), Stan Kaneshiki, and Ronald Takemoto (aiming the toy gun).

Two unidentified children hold court on their throne after being crowned the little prince and princess at the center.

A game of drop the handkerchief, led by center staff member Margaret Roberts, provides a bit of fun for a handful of the approximately 100 children who attended the facility daily.

Above, children, including Gene Nakata and "Charcoal" Nakamura, watch a staff member mix paints during arts and crafts time at the center. Below, children show off their own artistic talents using finger paints.

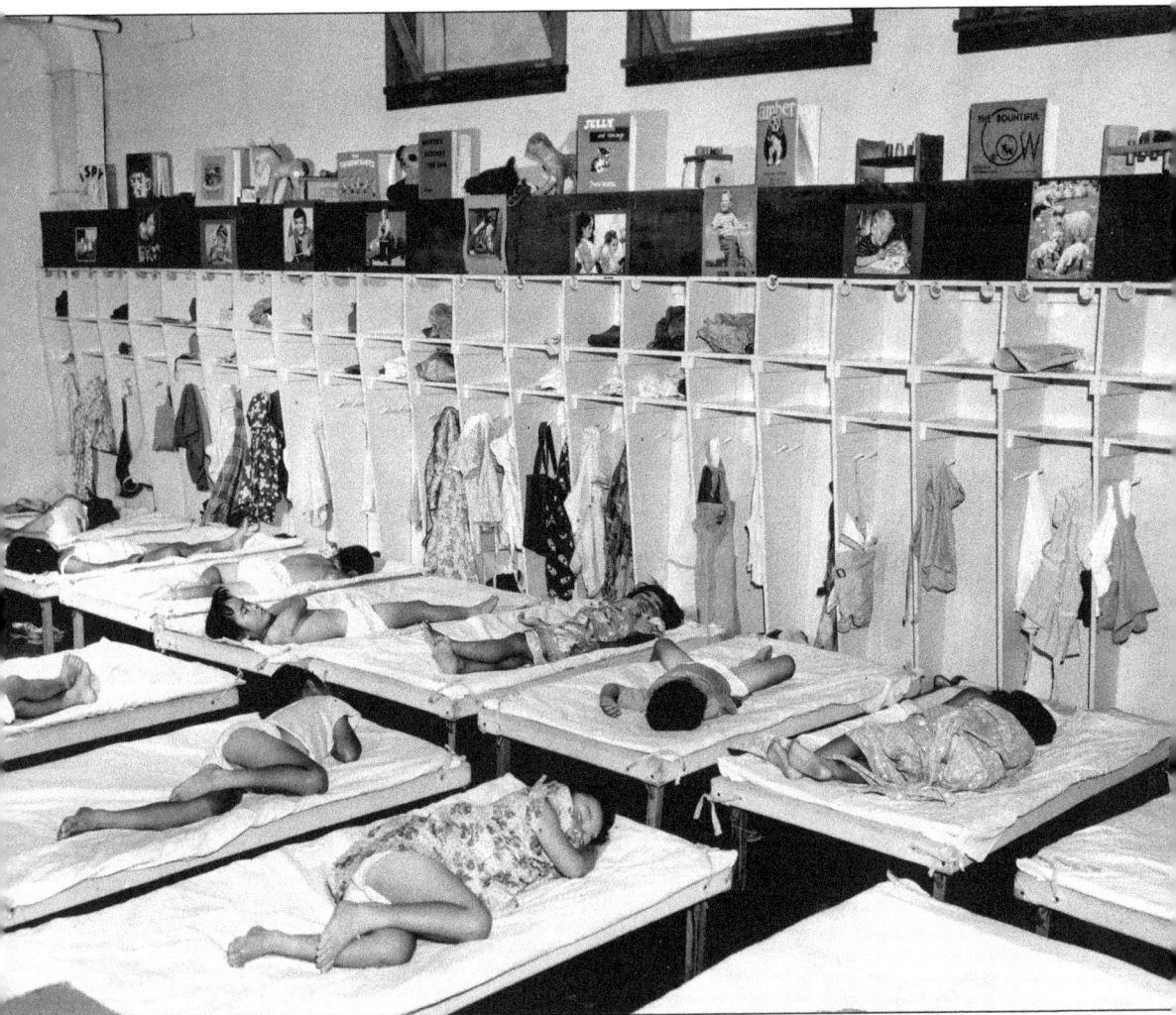

In addition to fun and games, children attending the center also took a 90-minute nap each day and awoke to a snack. Health and well-being were clearly important at the center, where in addition to the after-nap snack, children received a 10:00 a.m. snack, which included juice and cod liver oil, and a hot lunch.

Jack Seabrook poses with migrant workers' children alongside a sliding board in the day care center's playground during a visit. Seabrook was a member and long-term chairman of the New Jersey State Migrant Labor Commission.

Migrant workers' children listen to a childcare worker during story time at Seabrook's summer camp program in August 1951.

Wanting employees' children to be well educated, C. F. Seabrook established one of the first consolidated schools in a rural area in 1923, replacing four tiny schools that accommodated two grades each with a kindergarten–grade 8 facility. Teachers included, from left to right, (first row) unidentified, ? Logan, Louise Irvins (Price), unidentified, and Elizabeth Moore (for whom the school was later named); (second row) Alice Ware, three unidentified women, and Hazel Ranson; (third row) ? Myers, Eleanor Hackman (Craner), ? Fox, and ? Woodruff.

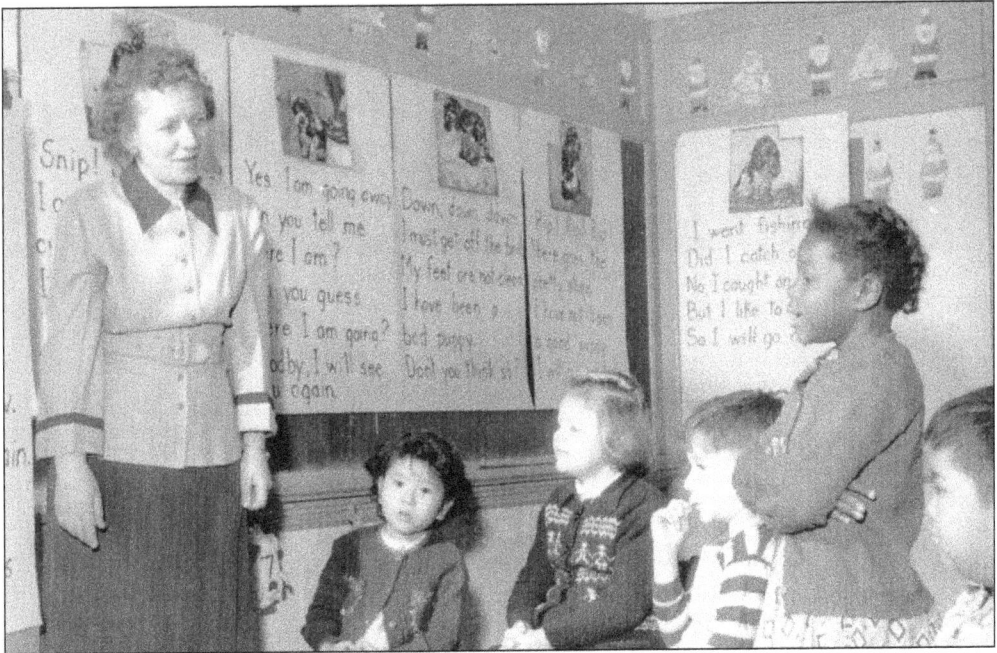

Seabrook School was integrated from its founding in 1923, educating the children of Seabrook employees as well as the children who lived on the company's contract farms. Here a Seabrook student stands to answer a question in Mary Croucher's class. Pictured students include Sumiko Oshio and Gary Sakamoto.

Seabrook School students proudly perform in a school production of the Buffalo Bill Rodeo on April 26, 1951.

A group of first graders put on the ritz during a class program around 1944.

Students perform the children's Christmas play on the stage of Seabrook School.

Frances Cowell accompanies the Seabrook School orchestra on the piano in June 1950. Orchestra members include Virginia Creamer, John Tice, Judy Cubberly, Neil Hetzell, Charles Cobb, Jean Matsui, Audrey Johnson, Bob Woodruff, Ogden Dickerson, Harry Hoffman, Frank Cloud, Eugene Morita, Stanley Kaneshiki, and Clarence Hemple.

Seabrook School students take part in the annual May Day parade.

Eleanor Craner's 1948 eighth-grade class poses in front of the Seabrook School. Class members include Marie Morano, June Inouye, Ruth Muraoka, Elaine Glaspey, Betty Ogata, Fujiko "Fudge" Ikeda, Hazel Okino, Mary Jean Mori, Donald Johnson, Frank Fox, Sam Yankelowitz, Donald Guth, Masaru Kazaoka, Larry Seabrook, Richard Stratton, Isamu Hashimoto, Albert Yano, Eleanor Craner, Ella Wease Seabrook, Olene Clark, Aileen Sharp, Thomas Van Meter, Douglas Nakamura, Hardy Fujiki, and David Nakauchi.

Fifth-grade students pictured here in 1947 include, from left to right, (first row) unidentified, Clifford Simpkins, Bob Woodruff, unidentified, Kenny Lang, Audrey Johnson, Jane Johnson, Marion Loew, Clara Minnick, Martha Blair, Jane Haaf, and Hazel Bentz; (second row) unidentified, Parker Fox Jr., Clayton Corson, Ed Rose, Jack Hildreth, Mary Moore, Elizabeth Akerboom, unidentified, Judith Cubberly, and unidentified.

Once through the eighth grade, students attended Bridgeton High School. In 1962, approximately 20 percent of the high school population came from Seabrook. As a testament to the success of Seabrook School educators, 6 out of 10 high school students who graduated with distinction that year were Seabrook students. Here, from left to right, Betty Hibbs, George Hanzawa, unidentified, Austin Gould, and unidentified concentrate on their science assignment at the high school.

Sports had a place in the life of Seabrookers of all ages. In this undated photograph, Jack Saunders oversees boxers in the ring at Seabrook.

Libby Crispin gets a hit during a game at the Seabrook Village field.

The Seabrook softball team, pictured here in July 1947, was tied for first place in the Bi-County Industrial League when this photograph was taken. Seated alone in the very front row is bat boy Ricky Kunishima. Team members included, from left to right, (first row) Wako Yokoyama, George Tsukashima, Ben Ogata, Lloyd Ide, Yosh Tsukamoto, and Mits Miyakawa; (second row) Jim Taniguchi, Seikyu Yamashiro, George Fuji, Shig Hiraki, Kaz Taniguchi, Walt Okamoto, and Ronnie Yonemoto; (third row) Displaced Persons personnel director Harold Fistere, Taro Yokoyama, Leslie Ozawa, Lefty Nishimura, Tosh Ichinose, Tom Murakami, Ben Matsumoto, Tee Saisho, and team manager Dick Kunishima.

Winning the league championship in 1948, Seabrook's men's softball team enjoys a moment in the spotlight atop a float in a Bridgeton parade. Players include, from left to right, Lloyd Ide, Leslie Ozawa, Walt Okamoto, Arthur Shibayama, Ry Yokoyama, Tom Murakami, and Lefty Nishimura.

Seabrook's first Jamaican cricket team poses for a photograph on the Seabrook School grounds.

Residents wait to board the company bus for a regular outing sponsored by Seabrook Farms. In addition to being the bus stop, the company's general store provided employees with a convenient place to shop for supplies. When families arrived at Seabrook with few belongings and no money, they often were given up to six months of free shopping at the store, as well as free meals at the company-run cafeteria.

Seabrook children prepare to take the plunge off the diving board at Parvin State Park in the early 1950s during a summer outing.

Workers' children pose in front of the community house for a photograph before leaving for a fun-filled day of summer camp at Clark's Pond. Generally at Seabrook, children under the age of 12 were provided with a range of social and educational programs rather than being relegated to the fields all day. Children age 12 and up were expected to work in the fields during their summer breaks from school.

Workers, dressed in their best, pose in the farm center between 1914 and 1920, possibly before heading off on an outing. The community house, located at Route 77 and Parsonage Road, sponsored a number of outings in warm weather, including trips to the shore, picnics, and fishing excursions. The house in the background was A. P. Seabrook's original farmhouse, where C. F. Seabrook lived in the early years of his marriage and where all four of the Seabrook children were born.

Members of Boy Scout Troop 47, sponsored by the Seabrook Japanese American Citizens League and Seabrook Farms, prepare a meal during their annual camping event.

Seabrook Girl Scouts enjoy canoeing at Parvin State Park during an outing. Irene Takemori mans the oar at the front of the closest canoe.

Seabrook Brownies huddle around their leader during a meeting.

Donning their Sunday best, construction paper hearts on their heads, Seabrook Boy Scouts pose for a photograph during a Valentine's Day social event sponsored by the troop.

Members of Seabrook's Cub Scout troop fool around during a meeting at the community house.

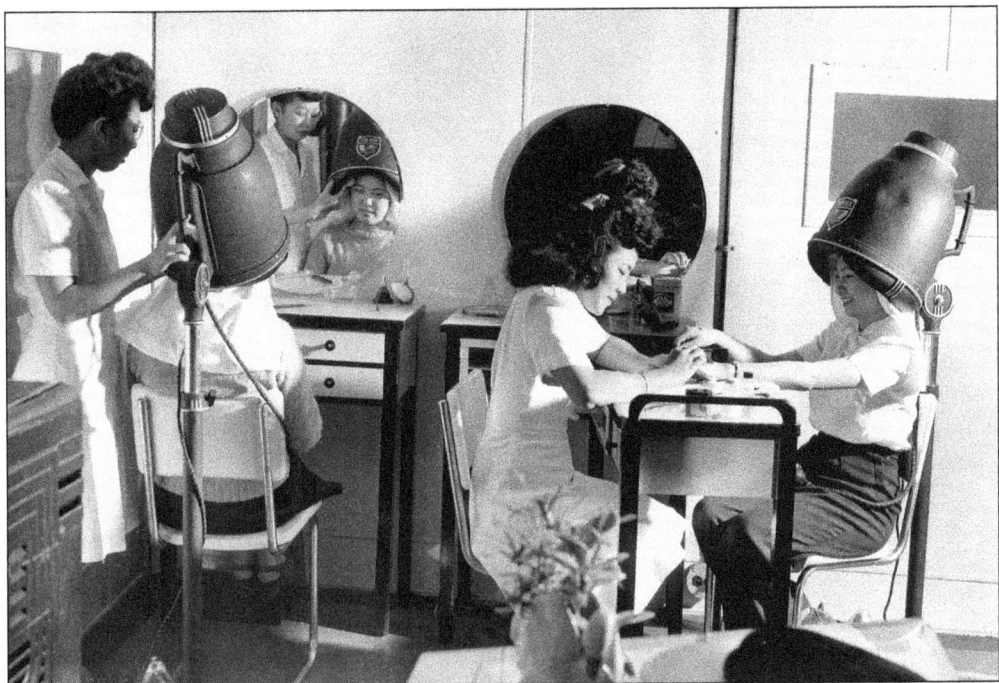

Beautician Esther Yamamoto Ono (left) adjusts the dryer on an unidentified woman, while Millie Yamashita works on Mary Nagao's nails at the Seabrook beauty shop. The women are preparing for an evening party, likely slated to be held at the community house.

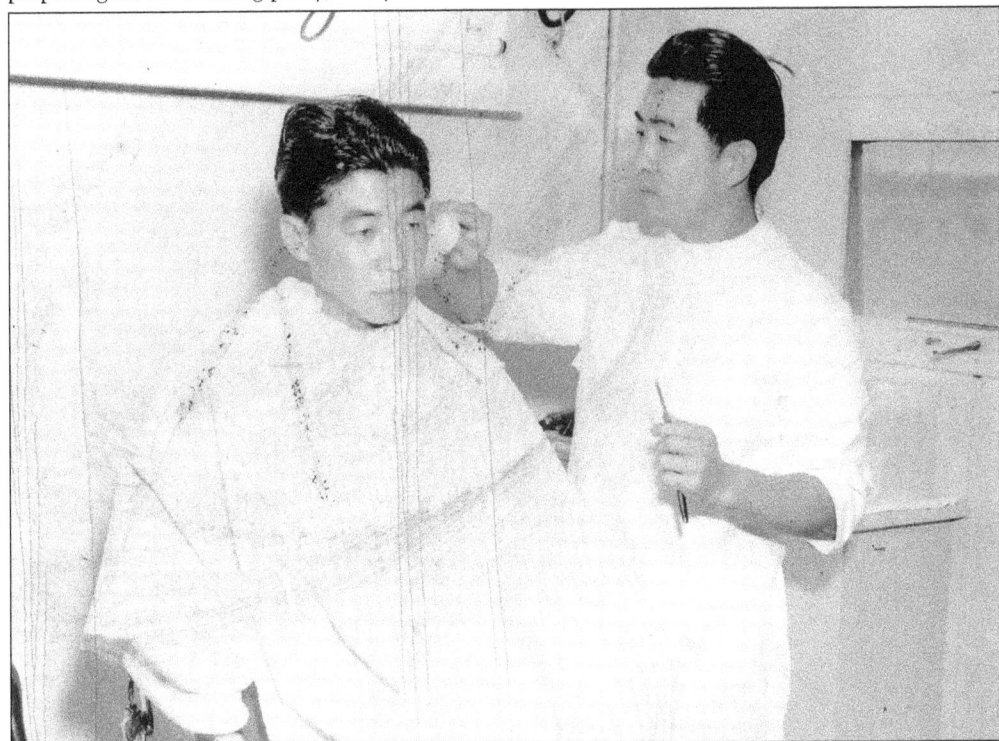

Seabrook barber Fred Ito takes a little off the top for an unidentified worker.

Two women leave the community house, where many of Seabrook's social activities took place. The housing office was located on the right, and the cafeteria, snack bar, lounge, library, social hall with a jukebox and dance floor, auditorium, and sports complex were on the left. The social hub of the community, workers paid 10¢ to see movies on Tuesday and Thursday nights. The United Service Organization (USO) operated the community house during World War II.

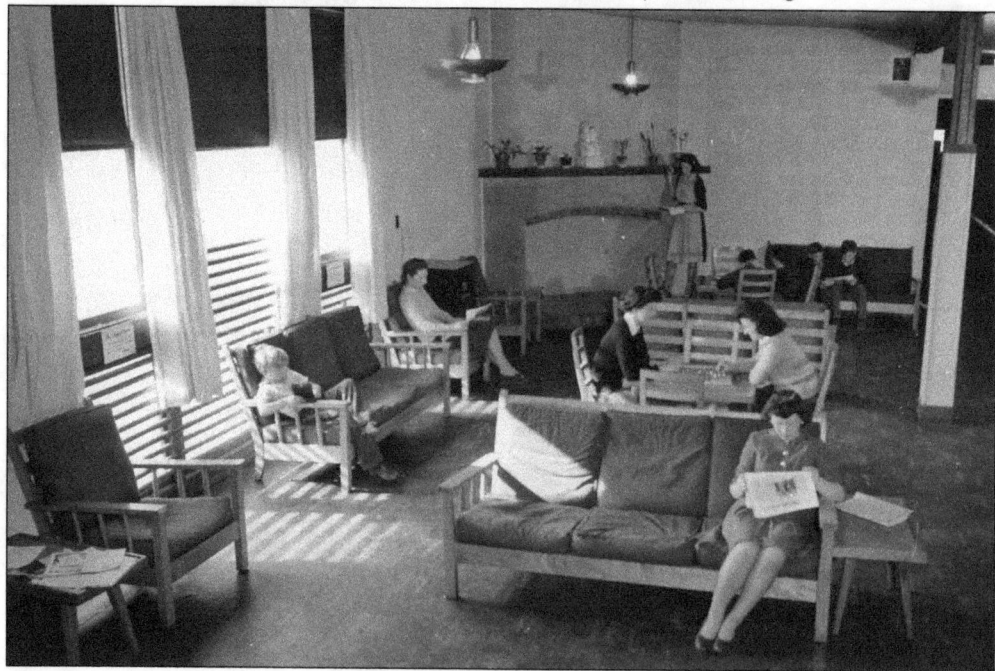

Seabrook residents relax in the community house lobby.

In order to keep production up during World War II, Seabrook ran a 24-hour walk-in cafeteria offering unlimited free coffee, soup, and sandwiches. Here workers select a meal from the cafeteria line in an undated photograph.

The snack bar was a favorite gathering spot for workers throughout the day. This photograph was taken around 1950.

Employees spend some free time browsing through the holdings at the free library located in the community house.

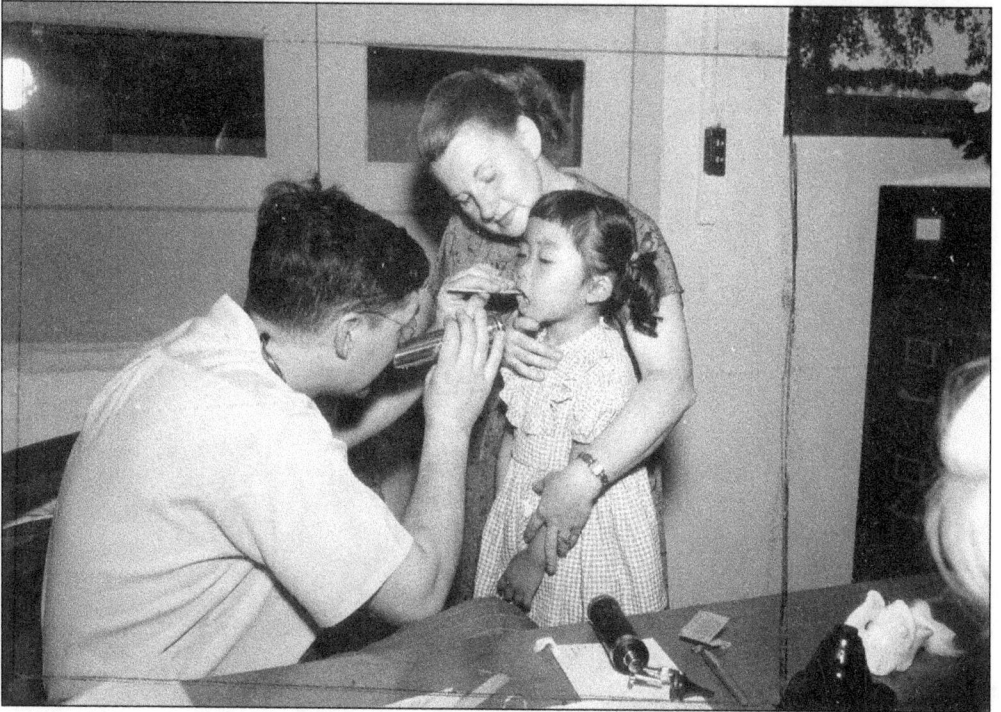

Janice Wadamoto says "ah" for Dr. Jonathan Moore during a routine physical examination of children in the childcare center.

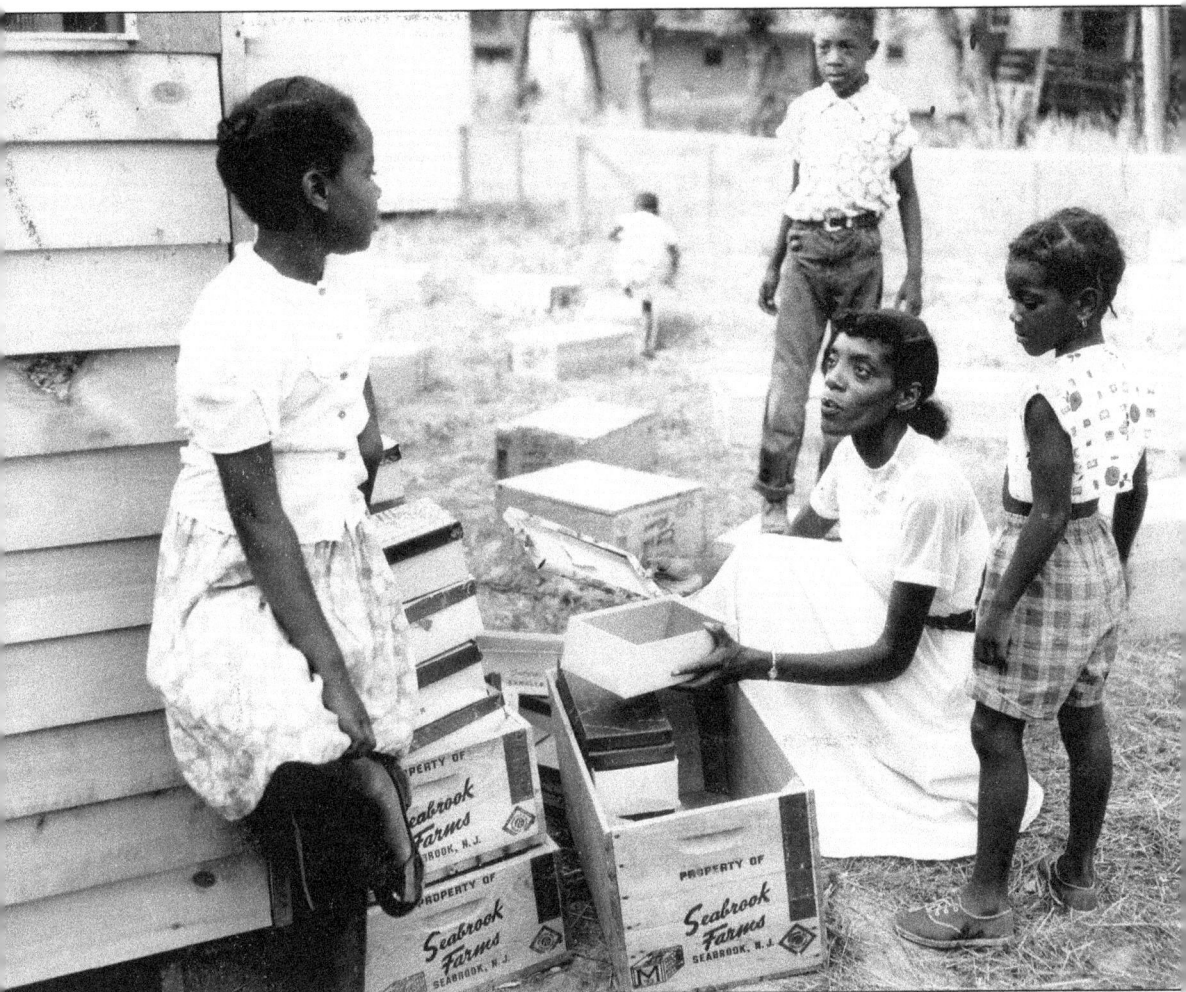

Migrant workers' children try on new shoes, provided by Seabrook Farms in July 1953.

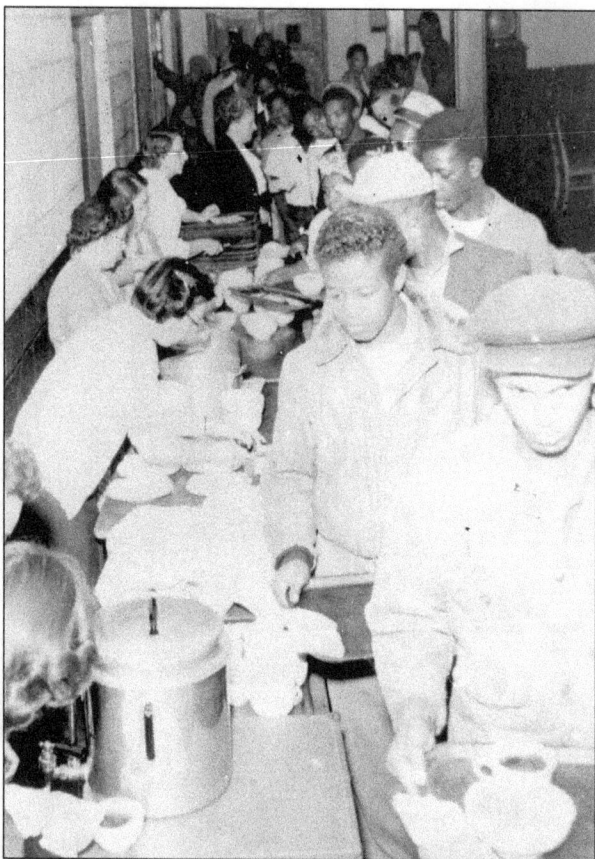

The community house was opened to more than just Seabrookers when the need arose. At one time it served as a temporary shelter for Delaware Bay flood victims following a nor'easter. At right, flood evacuees are served a hot meal by members of the Seabrook community. Below, babies settle in comfortably in their temporary surroundings.

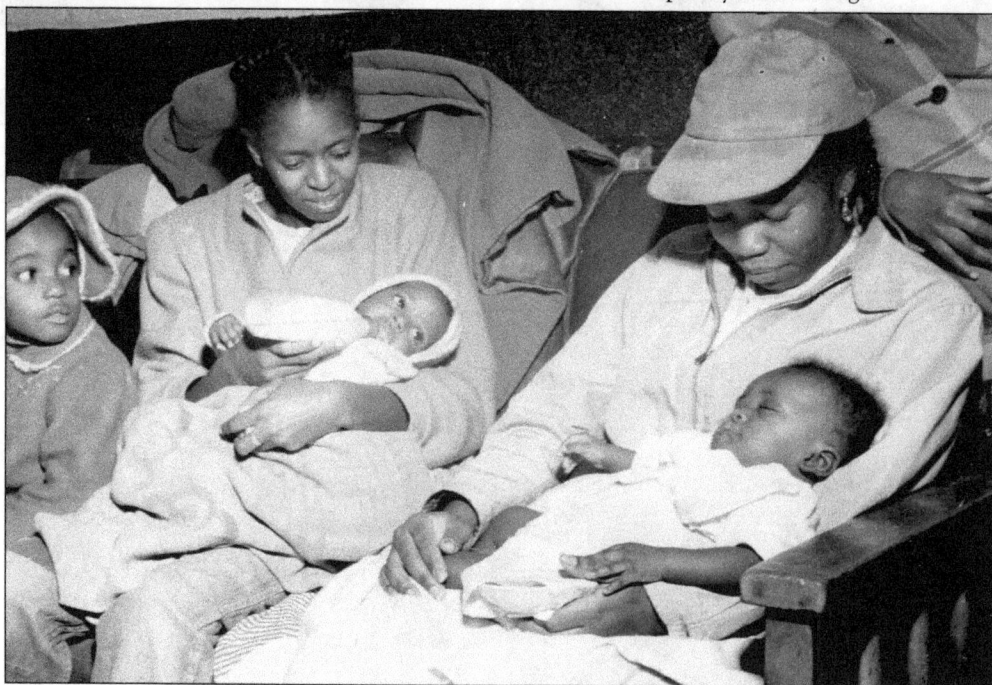

Members of the Seabrook family, as well as other company officers and supervisors, often visited with workers and their families for special occasions. In this photograph C. F. Seabrook (right) visits the childcare center with other executives and helps celebrate a toddler's birthday on July 25, 1951.

Jack Seabrook spends a moment with a new Jamaican baby, family members, and a nurse at the company's nursery on August 21, 1952.

A special event in the life of an employee or family member was a memorable moment for the whole community. In this photograph Seabrook women gather for a bridal shower.

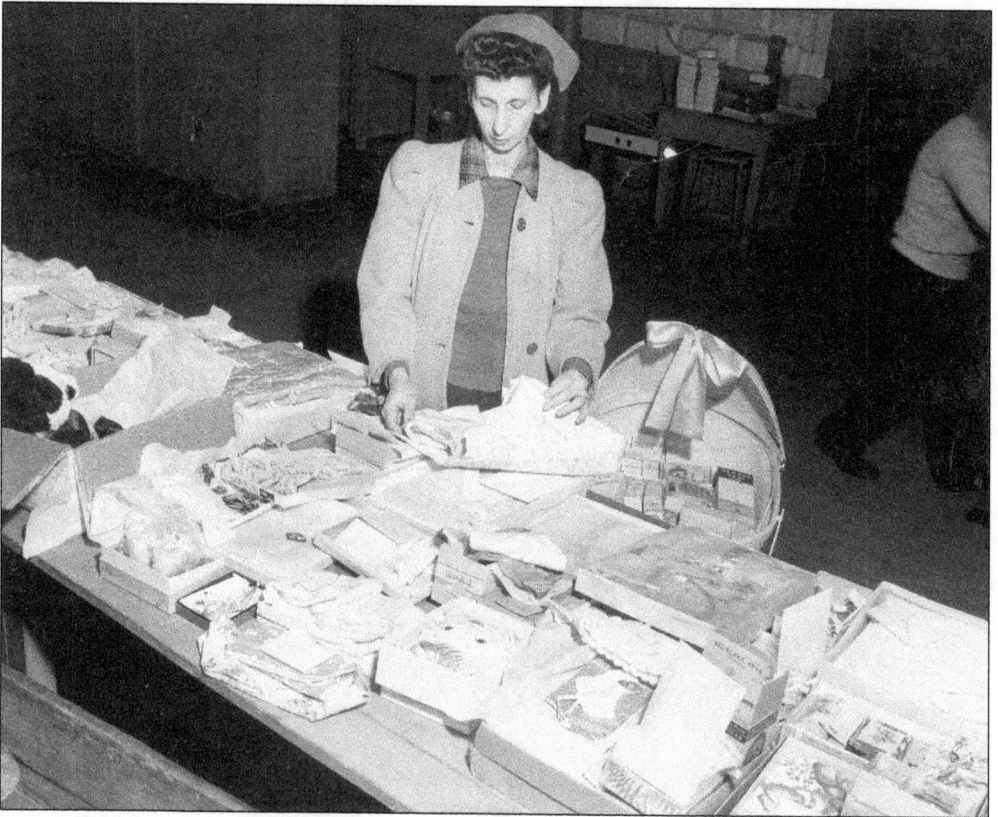

Dolores Carter, packing line supervisor, looks over her baby shower gifts.

The SEACO (Southeast Asian Coalition) Club performs a play at Seabrook School on December 2, 1953.

Santa Claus hands a little girl a bag of candy at the annual children's Christmas party at the community house on December 23, 1953.

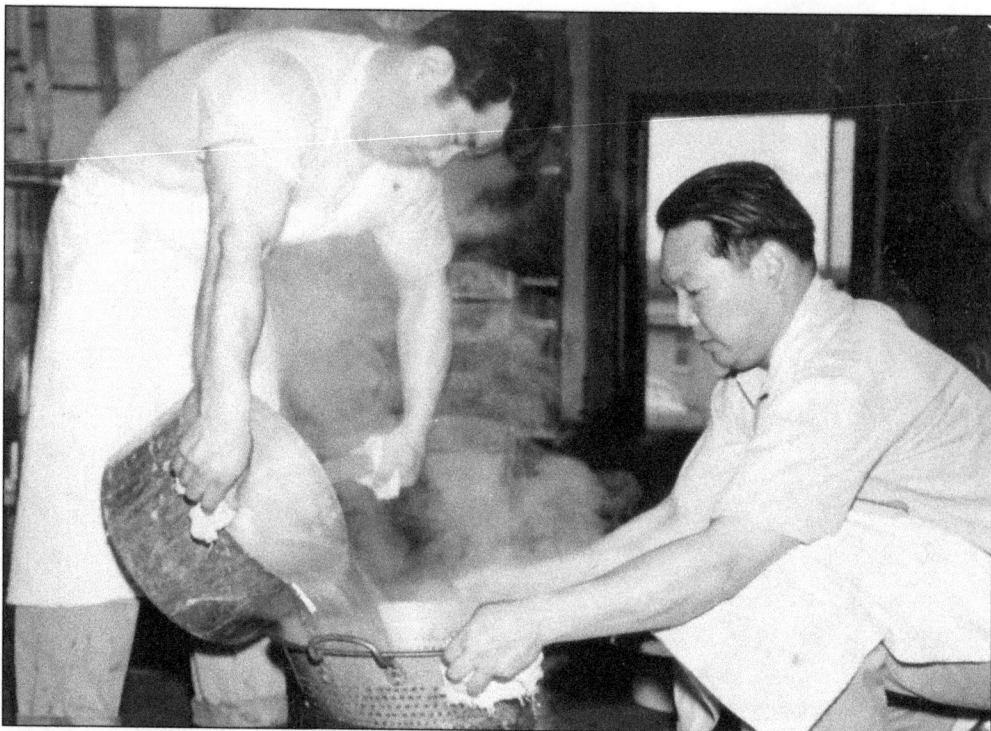

Takeshi "Sha Sha" Haijima and Dick Kunishima help prepare the annual charity chow mein dinner at the Seabrook School.

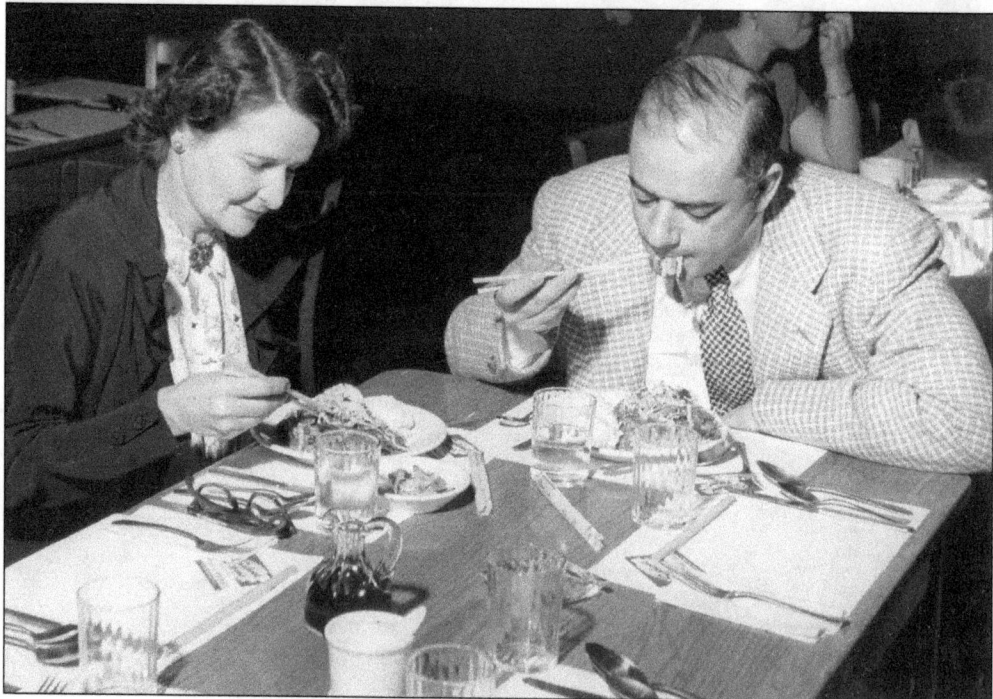

Community members dig into their chow mein before exploring the cultural exhibit and enjoying the entertainment that accompanied the annual event.

Talent shows at the community house always drew crowds. Here the Island Girls Chorus performs.

The Estonian folk dancing group poses for a photograph in 1956. Members included, from left to right, (first row) Mall Vabar, Riin Illisoo, Jaak Vilms, director Milli Poldma, Vello Erilane, Aili Abel, and Riina Poldman; (second row) Tiiu Kolts, Ivo Laurson, Tiina Upper, Vallo Truumees, Mare Runk, Hillar Palango, Mai Vilms, Juri Vilms, Saina Karp, and Jaan Kruus.

The Estonian a cappella chorus appears at the Seabrook community house in 1950. Over the years, the Seabrook group performed in numerous East Coast cities as well as Canada.

Couples celebrate at the annual harvest ball in this undated photograph.

A European band prepares to perform in 1952.

Mr. and Mrs. Harold Carlson take a turn strutting their stuff on the community house dance floor during a dance.

Visit us at
arcadiapublishing.com

www.ingramcontent.com/pod-product-compliance
Lightning Source LLC
Chambersburg PA
CBHW050552110426
42813CB00008B/2331